Riveting, raw honesty, inspiratio.
spiritually enlightening. Fred's willingness to share
so vulnerably about his marriage and journey through
cancer, depression, and brokenness will change your
life perspective. I needed every insight and word.

Robin Wood, *Consultant*

Fred does an incredible job of inspiring all of us as
he tells his story of how to move forward when life
throws you curveballs. Fred's authenticity, positivity,
and practical advice on how to move forward when
life doesn't go as planned is a must-read. You will be
inspired and motivated.

Andy Stephenson, *Ph.D. Campus Pastor*
Northview Church - Carmel, IN

An incredible story of uncertainty, faith, and hope!
A book that will give you the tools you need to
overcome your challenges and reach your full
potential. This is a book you need to read! Highly
recommended.

Mark Malin, *Multisite Director at Northview Church*

FREDTalk

Inspiration and Truth From a Friend

Fred Bays

HighFive
PUBLISHING

Fred Talk
Copyright @ 2019 by Fred Bays

Requests for information should be addressed to:
www.Fred-Talk.com

ISBN 978-1-7337692-9-7

Library of Congress Cataloging-in-Publication Data
Names: Bays,Fred 1970 – author.
Tile: Fred Talk / Fred Bays
Description: Ingalls, Indiana: High Five Publishing, [2017]
Identifiers: LCCN 2019914608 I ISBN 9781733769297

If you enjoy this book, please tell a friend! Because everyone can use a little Fred Talk: inspiration and truth from a friend!

To book a speaking engagement and for other resources visit www.Fred-Talk.com

This book is dedicated to:

Everyone who is currently in the fight against cancer, you are in my prayers!

All of you cancer survivors, we have a unique bond! God spared your life, so live it to the fullest!

Anyone struggling with depression and mental illness, you are not alone, there is hope I know you don't believe it right now, so borrow my faith for a while, let me help you see the light in the darkness you feel!

Whoever is stuck, searching for purpose in your life, let me in so I can show you how to replace that pain and limiting thoughts with life giving truths that will produce a future that is full of meaning!

And to the woman who has my heart, my bride, you have been my rock for over 30 years together! Thank you for walking through cancer, depression and career change with me! I love you forever Dyan, there is nothing we can't beat together!

FRED

Table of Contents

Prologue: So, what is Fred Talk?

I like to shoot straight with people and make things simple. Can we be honest with each other before you start reading my book? How many of you have had someone say something you didn't want to hear, but needed to hear it?

It's called truth.

But it's really hard to listen to when you don't like how it's delivered or feel like someone is being critical, or you don't feel like they care about you. We say things like, try to take the one grain of truth and forget everything else they said and did. Sounds good right? But it's hard to do! Can we agree that approach just isn't very productive?

Now let's talk about the other side of truth: love! How many of you have shied away from telling someone something hard because you care about them and didn't want to hurt their feelings? We all know that's not love; it's not grace! That's called wimping out! When we do that it's more about our own insecurities, right! Can we agree that approach doesn't help people either?!

Now that we are both on the same page; have you ever had someone that was a friend tell you something you didn't want to hear, but did it in a way that worked?

God often uses people in our lives to speak truth into us. When you know someone loves you, it's easier to hear! Sometimes we just need a friend that will tell us the truth! Somebody that we know believes in us, loves us, and can inspire us to become more.

My calling in life is to help you become the person that God made you to be; to unlock your full God-given potential so that you can produce the results that you want relationally and professionally. So when I say things that sting a little, please remember, my name is Fred, and I'm your friend!

In order for us to live at our full potential, we have to be able to identify the limiting beliefs that we have about ourselves. This starts with awareness! It's really hard to see the real picture when we are inside the frame! We're often stuck in our life just reacting to what happens. We have to learn how to step outside of the frame and work ON our life!

This requires that we take time to think about how we think. Most people live life not thinking about what they are thinking about. And then we get frustrated that our results are not what we want. The people who find success in any area of life learn the value of submitting to a coach. Great athletes, great business leaders, great marriages involve support and accountability!

We all need a mindset coach, someone that helps us see the true picture so we can learn how to remove limiting thoughts and become empowered to change our own lives! In order to hear some hard truths about ourselves, we have to remember that it comes from a place of love! Jesus never spoke truth without love. He also never spoke love without truth.

Throughout my book, you will notice that I talk about a lot of people that have made a significant impact on my life! Seventy-five different people are listed in this book!

We all need friends that speak truth in love to us! We need to learn from each other! This book is not about me! It's about you and your mindset! My story is just a tool I'm using to talk with you about life so you can hear it from a friend! I care about you and have prayed for you many times already! We may not have met yet, but we are friends!

So as you read my story, remember, my name is Fred, and I'm your friend!

SECTION ONE

WHAT EVERYONE FEARS

NO SYMPTOMS

I was in perfect health! I've always enjoyed working out, being an athlete. I'm a healthy eater and love my life! My teenage daughter, Chelsea, came in our bathroom one day and I had shorts on. She said, "Dad, that thing on your knee is gross, you need to get that cut off!"

I had a mole on the inside of my right knee that had been there for a while. I vaguely remember a few years earlier having a red spot that looked like a pimple and tried to pop it, but it didn't go away. I never thought about it after that. Even when Chelsea said something, I wasn't worried.

It just happens that the very next day I had to take my son Seth to the dermatologist for some warts he had on his hand. My wife, Dyan, had taken him numerous times to get warts frozen off. She had just started a new job as a school counselor after staying home for thirteen years with our kids and wasn't able to take Seth, so I took him.

At my son's appointment, Dr. Young had fun with Seth by spilling liquid nitrogen on the floor, causing a whisk of fog to move along the floor! After she finished freezing my son's warts, I asked her if she could look at something.

I told her my daughter didn't like how it looked and thought that I needed to get it removed. I asked the doctor if you can just cut moles off like mine. I was just inquiring for cosmetic reasons, thank God for teenage vanity!

Dr. Young looked at it and said, "I don't like the looks of this, either!" So she cut it off at my son's appointment! (Are you catching all of the God moments in this story yet?)

After we left the office, I didn't think much more about the doctor cutting off my mole. That was until one week later, when I received a call from Dr. Young, early on a Thursday morning.

My wife had already left for work, and I was getting out of bed when the phone rang. She was very kind and direct. The call lasted less than 3 minutes. I can remember it like it was yesterday! She kindly told me they got my test results back from the lab and then proceeded to tell me that I had Malignant Melanoma Skin Cancer and that I needed to have surgery to remove the rest. She gave me a phone number to call to schedule an appointment with the surgeon. My whole world changed in one 3 minute phone call!

Looking back on it, I can see God's hand clearly. Three times within a few days, things were lining up to catch my cancer when I had zero symptoms!

Let me stop for just a moment and say, we have no idea how God is working in our circumstances to guide us to bring about blessings in disguise!

I don't know if you believe in God or where you are in your personal views about faith and life, but I can tell you with crystal clarity that there is a Creator who loves you. He is at work in your life circumstances and wants to use everything that happens to you to help you understand your purpose for your life and His plans!

As you might imagine, when I first heard the words, I was in shock. I didn't know what to think. I just heard someone tell me I have Cancer.

For most people, Cancer strikes fear in them. It's a horrible killer! But you can't see it!

But aren't those the scariest things in life? The ones you can't see and aren't sure how to game plan for? It has a way of making us feel like we are helpless, even though we aren't.

I'll talk more about these feelings in the next chapter, but for now, I want to take a little time to unpack how the twists and turns in life are there to reveal things to us that we need to learn to pay attention to!

So here's where you might think I would start talking about how life circumstances change us. I used to think that until I read some books that opened my eyes to the reality that circumstances only have the power over us that we give them in our mind.

For most of us, we go through life with a victim mentality blaming bad things that happen to us for why our life is hard or has turned out the way it is. Let me share a truth with you that has changed my life and will empower you to become the person God made you to be no matter what happens to you in life!

Circumstances don't shape our lives; they simply reveal who we are! They are the litmus test for us to work out our character.

Remember my name is Fred, and I'm your friend! How we view, life is what determines our destiny, not what happens to us. We've all seen people who are faced with the same difficulties but end up with completely different results. Why is this? Is it luck? Is it chance? Is it favor?

What you believe will determine what comes of your circumstances. Please re-read that last sentence as many times as you have to until that truth sinks in.

We are so quick to jump to reasons or excuses for why our life turns out the way it does or why we respond the way we do to situations. But we're not actually thinking about it; we're reacting out of beliefs we have that reinforce what we think is truth!

For example, if you find yourself saying things like, "I can't control my our circumstances," then you have a belief that circumstances have power over you, so you end up throwing a bunch of pity parties because you feel helpless. And you make sure you tell everyone else about how unfair your situation is.

But what if you are simply creating that reality by what you believe about the situation? Could you be the one making your situation unfair? Is it possible that you are empowering the situation to hold you back?

Let me explain how this works by sharing one of my favorite card games! It's called: Euchre. I learned how to play in High School gym class in Ohio.

Whenever we had free time in class, which was most of the time, we would play Euchre. I learned to play with a kiddy, which is a pile of the extra cards that are not in the player's hands.

If you're unfamiliar, here's how the game is played: only five cards are dealt to each player. Then four are left hidden (these become the kiddy), and the top card is turned up for the dealer to either take or decline.

Round one everyone either passes or says pick it up to the dealer. If everyone and the dealer pass, then round two you can call whatever suit you want. I never liked playing this way because I could have a great hand but couldn't call the suit because a spade was turned up instead of a diamond, so I would have to pass while sitting with a hand that had the potential to take every trick!

Then I went to college and learned a different version of the game called: Bid Euchre. In Bid Euchre, you deal out the last four cards, and then each person bids how many tricks they can take. You are not limited to what card is turned up. You don't have to keep hoping everyone will say pass and then wait for everyone to pass again for you to blurt out the trump you want!

You have the power to influence the game immediately! This means you have to make more decisions quicker and can hurt or help your team more often. I personally like the ability to choose and influence every chance I get and live with the results; as opposed to sitting back and letting life decide for me and have to react to other people or situations being in control.

Most people live life thinking they don't have the power to change every circumstance they face. They hold their cards and wait for life to come to them and then complain about not getting the right cards dealt.

If I only had one more spade, I would have won that round! We live our lives explaining away why our life is not turning out the way we want it to. Always ending up on the losing side, a victim of the cards we were dealt! I want to propose that it's not the cards we are dealt that determine our results, but rather our beliefs. We go through life with a lot of limiting beliefs and don't even know it, because we are not taught how to think, we are taught what to think!

I've noticed that some people don't like to play Bid Euchre because "That's not the way you play Euchre." They get stuck on the rules they learned and like the limitations. There is a certain level of false safety in not having to make decisions and be responsible for every decision we make. It's much easier to just blame other people for why things go bad, whether it's a card game or life!

I'm known for taking a lot of risks in Euchre and life, but a risk is only a risk if you don't understand what is at stake and playing it safe and not stepping forward can be the biggest risk.

I believe God creates and allows circumstances that give us the opportunity for us to exercise our faith.

Our role is to believe in God and ourselves. Our actions in our circumstances demonstrate what we believe. Each time we face situations, it gives us an opportunity to step into the person God made us to be. How we choose to think about life creates new opportunities positively or negatively.

So I want to challenge you to learn to welcome every experience as a chance to grow and become what you think you can. You can't show your beliefs without circumstances!

YOU HAVE CANCER

Nobody wants to hear the words: "You have Cancer!"

They strike fear in the hearts of families! The word cancer is synonymous with death. It's a killer and causes so much hurt! I knew this about cancer because I had been a pastor for over 20 years and seen the pain many families went through and even watched my sister-in-law battle this terrible disease.

We've all seen it, but no one expects to hear those words referring to yourself! At first, I was in shock; it was surreal. I heard what the doctor said, but it wasn't registering.

Honestly, I never thought I was going to die. I felt like God had more for me to do. I wasn't afraid and viewed it as my next battle in life to overcome! So after I hung up the phone, I knelt down beside my bed, bowed my head and simply said, "I trust you!" Then I got up and went about my day.

One of the things I learned very quickly was that people who have cancer experience it on a different level than their family and friends. For those of us who have had cancer and gone through surgeries and treatments, we have a battle to fight. But for family members, they have a loved one they don't want to lose. I actually think it's easier for the person who has cancer because we are the ones it's happening to, and we are the ones who have to fight the fight.

I picked this up very quickly when people would see me; they would have this scared look on their face and didn't know what to say. They were afraid! People didn't know what to say!

I remember talking to one young guy who went to my church and worked in the medical field studying diseases, and he looked at me like I was going to die that very day. All he could say was I'm so sorry!

So I decided to confront it head-on and say the word a lot and not allow it to control us. I found myself assuring people; it's okay; we can smile and not let this dominate our thoughts.

There are certain things in everyone's life that you must work through on your own. Family and friends are huge, but if you are going to accomplish something significant in your life, then you have to do some personal work. You have to take responsibility for what you have to face. No one else can face what you need to face, and this takes some mental work. You have to decide what you want out of life and how you are going to view things.

What is it in your life that sets you back, scares you, intimidates you, and paralyzes you?

Is it relational stress? Maybe professional or financial uncertainty? Or maybe it's when people criticize you in some way? That's been a big one for me!

We all have a battle to fight where we have to work at mental focus so we can push through and not let situations become obstacles.

I often think of Jesus' words when people were afraid, oh you of little faith, if you had the faith as small as a mustard seed, you would say to this mountain move, and it would move![1] Jesus knew it all starts in our mind!

Everything starts in our mind! Everything we look at was created first in God's thoughts or our thoughts. Then that thought impulse vibrated us into action to make it happen! Mindset is everything because what we think about and believe is what we do! What you wish does not come true, only what you believe! We say we believe a lot of things, but our actions often show the opposite. Remember, my name is Fred, and I'm your friend!

Let me explain how beliefs and actions work. Our minds work like a computer; beliefs lie in our subconscious mind, which is our ROM memory. ROM memory is Read-Only Memory; it's long term stored data. Then we have our RAM, or Random Access Memory, which is our daily functioning conscious mind. We think with our RAM, but we draw on our ROM for our beliefs. We have stored data from experiences that we don't even realize we are accessing all the time.

Our ROM or subconscious mind is shaped early in our life. According to Bruce Lipton, a cell biologist and author of The Biology of Belief, our beliefs are formed from the third trimester in the womb until about five to seven-years-old when our faculty of reasoning develops. [2]

Until then, all of our long term files are created by our parents and environment. These files develop two different ways:

1. Sudden impact, when a deeply emotional experience happens that cements in our brain a belief about that type of situation, often this is formed from fear.

2. Space Repetition of Time, repeated experiences over and over form habitual thoughts that control our actions. Repeated daily affirmation or rejection cement beliefs in our mind also.

Now, before you go blaming your parents for all of your shortcomings, you are NOT a VICTIM! If you believe it's everyone else's fault, it's because you have a belief that you are powerless. That's just not true.

Remember, my name is Fred, and I'm your friend! You are allowing yourself to believe a lie. We all have insecurities and fears and difficult situations, but how we view them is what determines our success or failure. Because the truth is, we have the power to change our own mind and beliefs!

But the problem is, we ALL have CANCER! And I'm not just using the word as a metaphor for bad thinking!

When I was diagnosed with cancer and talked with doctors and read the information, I realized that we all have cancerous cells in our body. These cells are cells that are defective and unhealthy. We don't have a problem until they metastasis, or come together; that's when we get told we have cancer by a doctor.

The reality is these cells are constantly looking for the right environment to grow. I'll talk more about how these cells mutate in a later chapter and what they are looking for that cause them to grow. But for now, I want you to realize that there are negative and limiting thoughts in your mind that are lies. They are lies that you believe about yourself, others, life, and God. And they are cancerous! If you aren't careful with your thoughts, they will form into beliefs that can destroy your life.

When negative thoughts are left alone, they destroy marriages, families, health, careers, finances, and your spirit. As a pastor and sports coach my whole life, let me be your Mindset Coach so we can win the Championship for your life!

Maybe it's time for a little elementary science lesson. I've taught 4th grade and STEM the past five years, so this will be very practical!

We all know that life is made up of two things: matter and energy.

All matter is moving or vibrating. The atoms and molecules that make up a table are so dense they cannot move freely, but if you heat the table up, they will begin moving.

Liquid atoms are constantly moving to take the shape of whatever container it is in. The majority of our body is made up of water. Our brain is almost 75% water; even our bones have 30% water. We have energy flowing through our body constantly. That's why they can hook wires up to us and do an EKG.

Nothing new yet right? Basic stuff we all know! Now, think about this! Our thoughts are just vibrations of energy, either positive or negative. We all know that our mind controls our body. So what we dwell on eventually we will do.

Our vibrations of thought express themselves through our body, acting on it. We all know this. You can feel the vibe when you walk in a room. When we are really mad most of us either yell or hit something. When we are really happy, we laugh and jump up and down.

But what makes us mad and happy? When external vibrations from others collide with our beliefs. We affect one another! We transfer energy back and forth. Our brain is our receiving station that processes the vibrations of energy. And it accesses our subconscious mind without us even knowing it, to tell us if we like or dislike the vibration.

And get this, whatever vibration we are putting off, attracts the same vibration. I hate my teacher, so do you? Oh, you're my friend! My boss sucks, oh, you think our boss also sucks, let's talk about him more and see if we can find other people who agree with us! Or I'm going to impact the world for good today, oh, you are focused on positive change also, let's do it together! Whatever we think about magnetically attracts the same vibration. So we literally create our destiny by our thoughts. RE-READ that!

This is why God says in Proverbs 4:23, more than anything you guard, protect your mind, for life flows from it! In scripture, our mind and heart are connected. Our emotions come from our heart or mind. We say think from your heart. We have to understand the power of our mind to create our life. God says in Proverbs 23:7 (KJV) As a man thinketh in his heart, so is he.

So let me say it again, and maybe it will sink in this time! You have CANCER!

There are negative, destructive, cells in your body that have the potential to form together and ruin your life. You have negative and limiting thoughts in your heart that will grow and develop unless you remove them!

Most illnesses start with negative thoughts: doubt, stress, worry, fear! As your thinking doctor, I am giving you my best advice; remove those negative cancerous cells from your body!

You have the ability to surgically remove the bad cells in your body and replace them with healthy, positive, life-producing cells! It all starts with AWARENESS! Admitting that I'm being fearful, critical, self-absorbed is the first step. Religiously speaking this is our sin nature, our tendency to distrust and blame others, even God. So I better protect myself at all cost. This destroys us over time; it destroys us mentally, relationally, emotionally, physically, and spiritually. God wants to free us from these destructive ways of thinking!

The issue is, most of us continue to believe we don't have a problem with how we think. People say, "I don't believe negative things! I trust God! I love people!" Then make excuses for why they constantly criticize their spouse, blame others, and worry about all sorts of issues in their life.

We are creatures of habit; if our habits are negative, we will tell ourselves and others why our habits are okay, it's called self-preservation. We're all human and make mistakes, that's true, but it's not an excuse for allowing ourselves to live a life full of excuses.

People know we're going to mess up; it's so refreshing to deal with people who just own their mistakes, make amends, learn from it, and stop repeating it! It's called forgiveness! When we learn to quickly forgive ourselves and others, we can get on the other side of the equation: the solution side!

People in society tend to be very forgiving if someone genuinely owns their mistake and corrects it because we all know that we're prone to make mistakes! God also knows this, remember, He created us! And because He's a loving Father, He went first and offered forgiveness because relationships matter deeply to him! It's in his character!

I don't know your experience with religion and God but know this, God loves you and demonstrated this truth by sending his son Jesus Christ to die for you so that you could be saved or restored to God's original design!

We were created without cancerous cells, pure, in the image of God, and He said we were good. The story of Genesis talks about our downfall when we believed a lie that God was holding something back from us; He gave us one limit, don't try to play God and control everyone.

Look it up in Genesis 3; He said you can eat from every tree but one, the Tree of the Knowledge of Good and Evil. If you eat from it, you will die. What we put in our mind either produces life or death friends! Humanity chose control, mistrust, self, and death.

Why did we choose to reject our creator's advice? We were deceived by his enemy Satan, who lied and said you won't die if you eat from that tree, you will become like God! Be very careful in life who you take your advice from; Satan tried to overthrow God and lost; he's bitter!

Be very careful around bitter people who need to be in control of everyone! Are you tracking with me friends? You may not believe the story of Genesis, and that's okay if you don't, but I would bet something in your spirit is resonating with the truth of how I'm describing life plays out! So come along on a journey with me and let's discover where positivity and negativity come from!

I'll talk a lot more about this mindset stuff in the section of the book titled Fred Talk, but for now, please trust me, YOU HAVE CANCER, get rid of every CANCEROUS cell in your body now! Change your beliefs so that you can think life-giving thoughts!

HOMECOMING

The day I got the phone call that I had cancer was Homecoming weekend. My daughter, Chelsea, was 15 and was so excited to go to her first Homecoming with her boyfriend Jacob, who is now her husband! She already had her dress picked out, and my wife Dyan was so excited to share this moment with Chels that I couldn't spoil the weekend! So I kept the news to myself!

My wife and I share everything with each other. We are open books and have always been best friends and soul mates. We support each other when the other is struggling and celebrate every chance we get. We've been married for twenty-seven years and dated for three years before that. So we have been through a lot of life together. I knew how Dyan would respond when I told her the news. 20 questions! That's the game she always plays with people!

My wife is naturally reserved and contemplative. She is an S on the DISC personality assessment. S's are very stable, loyal, and slow to change. They are the backbone of our society. 70% of people are S's. They are very protective of family! You don't mess with mamma bear!

My family likes to make fun of me for always talking about people and their DISC "letter". I've always been fascinated with personal growth and assessments. As a football coach and offensive coordinator at heart, I love to position people in their strengths so teams can produce the most points! I love to see people excel at what they do best! That's why I became certified in the DISC assessment to help organizations and families see how people are wired and how to best relate and position for the best results!

I can remember when Dyan and I went on our first date after having our daughter Chelsea. I was so excited that we were finally getting time together again, but like many new mothers, Dyan spent most of the time worried and thinking about if Chelsea was going to be okay.

So I knew that if I told Dyan I had cancer, it would have a similar effect, and cause the weekend to have a dark cloud over it. She wouldn't be able to enjoy the experience with her daughter! So I decided to wait until after I met the doctor the next week. Then I would have answers to the 20 questions and would be able to lead my family rather than struggle to help them and myself.

It was a new experience for me to deal with something this big privately and still engage with my family like everything is good! It made me think of all the veterans who go to war and fight horrible battles and at the same time, mentally have to engage their families in their world.

It made me think of Jesus who knew he was headed to the cross to die for the sins of the world to redeem humanity and yet he was fully present with his disciples even hours before his death. He actually knew the entire time he was blessing people and restoring health and teaching what was going to happen and even tried to explain it a few times, but his followers never got it.

There is a truth I discovered that weekend! We all have pain and fears and challenges that only we can face. How we manage that reality shapes our closest relationships and life. We can get mad at everyone around us and blame everyone else out of fear and hurt, telling everyone how they just don't understand the stress we're under; or we can find peace and security in the midst of our deepest struggles that gives us confidence and courage.

I don't know what your views are on God or faith, but I have a little different take than most people. Most Christians talk about faith in Christ as if you can only be Godly if you are weak and broken. I don't see it that way. I believe God wants us to live from a position of strength and wholeness.

Yes, we all need Christ because, without his perfect sacrifice, we all deserve death. We're sinful; we are selfish; God is love. Every day I thank God for saving me because of what Christ did on the cross. But there is so much more to our faith beyond that!

I believe God redeemed humanity for the purpose of accomplishing His purposes here on earth now. Bad news and difficult circumstances don't have to weaken us or break us! When I look at humanity – I see God when I watch people face life with courage whether they believe in God or not! And if you are a believer ... God says you are a new creation!

I believe putting God first in all you do is the highest purpose in life and practice that truth and experience many of God's blessings because of living that way, but I also experience a lot of difficulties because of that truth and I am ok with that!

I believe God allows us to have a certain level of meaning and purpose in life, whether we acknowledge Him or not. I've seen a lot of people who are very fulfilled in their marriage or career but who don't live for God. And I've seen a lot of people who work really hard at being spiritual and have lousy marriages and are not fulfilled in their work. I have a lot more to say about this, but I will save it for my next book – *Everything is Spiritual*. Truth and faith can be found outside of the church. Not all spirituality is true, but learn to be open to affirm it wherever you see it!

I'm very passionate about sharing good news, because people find god through us! I love to help others discover the truth of the gospel and turn their life over to God. I've had the privilege of leading a lot of people to put their faith in Christ. I believe that God is ALWAYS at work in this world and in people's lives, and I like to help point that out from a positive viewpoint rather than focus on the negative.

When I read the Bible, I see a love story of God speaking hope and life into the world, that he has a positive future he is moving us toward rather than focusing on what is wrong. I believe you can find God in both failure and success.

It's kind of like parents or bosses who always have to make sure their kids or employees know they were wrong and how wrong they were and how right the authority figure was. I have found that my kids and employees and people, in general, tend to sense when they are off and are often embarrassed, there is no need to drag people through the mud and make them feel worse about themselves, help them see what positive step they can take forward.

So, I think a lot of people are somewhat content in life, but there is so much more. And if that is all people want is to be content in this life that is all they get. But living for this life is missing the biggest truth about life, that we were created for eternity, not temporary fulfillment. We were created in the image of God, who is eternal, so we will live for eternity. So to live this life for now and not acknowledge the reality of our creator and live for him means we are choosing to reject him. Our creator holds the keys to eternity, and he has shown us the doorway of his son Jesus Christ. It's up to us to accept this truth and walk through the door to a new eternal life with our creator.

This chapter is about sharing bad news. Many people are afraid to talk about hard things, we don't want to offend people and end up allowing ourselves and others to shrink back. So can I share some bad news with you in an inspiring way?

There is a hell (bad news), there is also a heaven (good news). They are real. We get what we want and choose. God doesn't send people to hell; He loves people, we choose whether or not we believe in a loving creator who has prepared a beautiful place for us for eternity with meaningful work to do and loving relationships or to reject that. If God is life, love, and truth, then the opposite of God is death, hate, and a lie. I don't want you to go through this life, believing a lie that there is no eternal life in heaven or hell. It's not hateful for God to have a heaven and hell; it's actually in his character of love and truth to abide by the laws of nature he created, cause and effect. He created heaven. Satan, God's enemy created hell. Don't allow yourself to be deceived that God is mean; God will make sure evil does not win! We get what we want or choose. So choose wisely! Choose to receive true life today by admitting your sin and turning from it to God. Our gracious God offers forgiveness and eternal life.

If you are a believer focus on the good news of hope that Jesus Christ offers our world. We don't have to be discouraged when we hear people talk about sin because it's only as strong as we make it. Once we accept Christ, God empowers us by his Holy Spirit to live life for his purposes. We are good; we are loved, accepted, and secure. So now we have a ton we get to do for and with him until we go to heaven.

I don't know about you, but that excites me. Because I want my life to count now, I want to do a lot of things, I want to accomplish some great things, and this includes career, money, and influence. And this is not bad or selfish. We either do a lot for ourselves or for God. As I read through scripture, there are lots of people who wanted to do great things for God, and they did. They had confidence in who they were and were able to face challenges with courage.

I remember talking with a good friend of mine one day, Kent Jones; he was recovering from open-heart surgery at the same time I was recovering from cancer. He is my age, and we had played a lot of basketball together, he was in good health, but his dad had a heart attack and major blockage at 40 and had to have open-heart surgery so he went for a checkup just to be safe and they found major blockage! The Doctor told him he was a walking time bomb for a major heart attack!

Kent and his wife Shawnda were one of the first friends we made when we moved to Pendleton 15 years ago. Our sons were in 1st grade together, and they hit it off! Their son, Parker, has always been small and my son, Seth, was big, so we called them Mutt and Jeff! Parker now runs at Notre Dame, they are still great friends and even lived together this past summer in Indy. Shawnda has horses, and Dyan grew up showing Quarter Horses, so they had a lot in common. Kent and I loved sports.

Kent did not grow up in the church; he travels around the world for his job. I remember saying to him; God was watching out for you. I asked him if he sees how God worked in that situation. He went on to share with me that as an engineer, he tends to see things differently. Then he shared something that stuck with me. He said, I just don't relate to the message I hear from most Christians, it seems so negative, that we have to find God in weakness. Then he said, but I don't feel like you come off that way.

Something clicked in my mind when Kent said that! Just because you find God in your weakness doesn't mean that's the only way to find Him! And I have spent a lot of time researching this, and I have found that many Christians do not feel very self-confident, yet they are supposed to feel loved and forgiven. Why is this? They have a view of themselves that is disempowering, and that seems to set them up for consistent failure; like it's bad to be confident in yourself or as if it's a sin or selfish to have a strong, healthy self-image. So if someone who is not a believer hears us talk about God, we are often critical of qualities that are good in them rather than helping them see how God is at work in their lives from a positive perspective.

When I pray for my friends who don't have a personal relationship with Christ and talk with them, I often see how they would make an incredible impact for the Kingdom because they already have a solid foundation of character and stability in their life. Kent and his wife Shawnda have a great marriage of over 25 years. They manage their money well. They are some of the most genuine and relationally adept people I know! And Kent is hilarious! Why does someone have to find God when things are bad? I see God's character at work in them. I believe strength and positivity is a much more attractive approach and has a deeper lasting effect! We all know that we are not God and that we mess up. I believe focusing on our hope versus our problem was Jesus' approach.

If you're reading this and right now thinking that Fred waters down the truth of the Gospel, you better re-read how frankly I have already written the truth of our sin and need for God's forgiveness. I have John 14:6 Jesus is the way, the truth, and the life; no one comes to the Father except through his son tattooed on my skin! I am asking Christians to reframe your belief system, so it doesn't just sound like a bunch of BS to the world! Quit focusing on weakness and everything that is wrong! Remember, my name is Fred, and I'm your friend! Jesus said to the woman caught in adultery, the sick, the cheating businessmen, go and sin no more, your faith has healed you! You are now good in my eyes, so let's get on with the purpose of your life! As I look at many Biblical leaders, I don't see them all finding God in weakness, Samuel, Joshua, David, and Barnabus, to name a few.

Marcus Buckingham is one of my favorite speakers and authors. He is an expert in researching what produces strength. He lets the facts reveal the truth. I love that! He's not a believer, but he's always searching for the truth! His book StrengthFinder2.0 is a bestseller that helps you discover your strengths. He is famous for asking parents, if your child comes home with all A's and one F on their report card, which subject should your child focus the most time on? The majority of parents say the F. Studies show that's wrong! It's focusing on what they will never do well and robs them of exponential growth in an area of strength. Marcus finds the same problem in businesses as he works with Fortune 500 companies. We are fixated on our weaknesses, the bad news. It will NEVER produce strength or confidence! But we continue as a society to indoctrinate this belief system. I am VERY passionate about this subject and have another book in me on this topic! I have a chapter later that touches on this truth that positivity always wins! Please, hear me on this one! We don't grow focusing on what is wrong in ourselves and others, God doesn't work that way with us, that is a lie from the enemy who hates God and uses the approach of accusing and skepticism and negativity to steal our joy, kill our hope and destroy our confidence!

If you're worried that this mindset of focusing on the positive versus what's wrong won't produce solid believers who grow in their faith, the real test is to see the fruit of our labor. Every time I think of my dear friends Brian and Staci Inskeep my heart is so full of gratitude for how God allowed me to play a small part in leading them to faith in Christ. Brian was an atheist who founded a multimillion-dollar electrical design company called InPwr, Staci was told that God couldn't use her as a worship leader because of her divorce. It was almost 15 years ago when I met them and what a joy to baptize Brian with his daughter and have Staci leading our worship services! And Brian uses his own personal plane to fly his team to help with disaster relief efforts for multiple days even though his company is now in multiple states around the country!

Then I think of Tim and Kristi Day, who have been dear friends for almost 20 years now! Kristi prayed for Tim, who wanted nothing to do with God for years, I can't tell you how rewarding it is to see Tim help fund mission work in Africa for orphans and hear Kristi share about her annual trips overseas! Those are just two of our special couples who were strong individuals that were attracted to the positive mindset they saw in our church. And God's spirit has continued to grow their faith!

A lot of people are not sure how to grow their faith. So I have created three Faith Surveys that you can take online in less than 5 minutes that will help you see where you are at in your Faith in God, yourself and others. Just go to **www.Fred-Talk.com** and click the link Faith Survey. This will help you see where you are at right now in each area and then I will have resources that will give you some steps you can take to tangibly grow your faith in each area.

If you have a strong belief in God and low self-worth, you shrink God to your level. If you don't love and believe in people, you use them. We're supposed to save people! Those of us who have a strong self-image and low view of God tend to mislead people for personal gain. Our belief system creates our life! So it's really important that we have positive, life-giving beliefs about God, ourselves and others. Make sure you're beliefs aren't a bunch of BS!

Remember, my name is Fred, and I'm your friend! It's Homecoming weekend; God has some great plans in store for you. Are you going to let some bad news about your health, challenges at work, or what someone said to you ruin your weekend plans?

It's all in how we frame it my friends! You're not alone; we all face tough stuff, let God encourage and empower you to handle it with grace and confidence! Marriage can be difficult, Dyan and I have had some rough patches, but it's worth sticking through and getting to the backside of things, because you grow and learn and are blessed for it! Some marriages are harder than others, that doesn't mean it can't become something great! The goal in marriage is not happiness; it's faithfulness. Faithfulness takes work, forgiveness, love, … I'm happily married and love my life, but I also work at both!

I had one of my mentors as a pastor tell me a long time ago, Dave Rodriguez, who pastors Grace Community Church, you have to learn to live with a low-grade fever of sadness. There will always be things that are sad that you might not be able to change, but don't let that dominate your life. I used to listen to what people tell me, the older I get; the more I don't pay attention to what people say, but rather what they do! So that's why I can see God and spirituality in people who may not acknowledge God and why I don't agree with what every person who says they are a Christian says, even if it sounds nice. It's Homecoming weekend, live like it!

20% CHANCE TO LIVE

It was the fall of 2011 when I was told by the doctor that I had a 20% chance to live past five years; talk about some hard words to hear! Well, I sure blew those odds away!

I had a very serious form of cancer that is known to kill fast! Malignant Melanoma, stage 3 was my diagnosis. Stage 4 is very serious. It is your internal organs, and you are as good as dead unless God miraculously heals you. The only way to get rid of Malignant Melanoma is to surgically remove it. There is no real treatment to try to kill it.

I sat in the doctor's office by myself as he laid out the harsh realities of my form of cancer. He told me he was going to cut a football-shaped size out of the inside of my knee because it was so deep into my skin. Then he was going to test my nearest lymph nodes in my right groin to see if it had spread and would send that to pathology.

He recommended I then take an experimental drug called *Interferon*. At the time, it was the only drug they had, and it only showed that it reduced the chances of the cancer coming back by six months. There was no strong evidence it would do anything, but it's all they offered. It is a very potent drug that wreaks havoc on your mind and body over time. I'll share more about my experiences with this treatment in the next section of the book.

After the doctor laid out the realities, he asked me very matter-of-factly, "Do you have any questions?" I said yes, I have one question. What advice would you give in how to break the news to your wife and kids?

My doctor was the best malignant melanoma plastic surgeon in the region; he was very blunt, so no pastoral bedside manner. But I was okay with that because I didn't need a nice guy. I needed someone who was confident in removing the cancer. His reply to my question was, "You should have had your wife here with you today!"

WOW! Talk about a slap in the face! But if I had to do it all over again, I would do the same thing, because as you'll hear in the next chapter, I was prepared for every one of the 20 questions. And I was able to answer them in a much softer tone, which was very helpful! But before we move on to me breaking the news to my wife and kids, let me share a few thoughts with you about bad news, health, and doctors.

We all hear some bad news eventually! You did not make the basketball team. We have to let you go from your job! It's not working out; I want a divorce! I hate you, mom! You're dad died! You have a blockage and need heart surgery!

Let's just be honest, bad news sucks! None of us like it! But it's a natural part of life! Until we accept the reality that bad news is part of life, we will constantly waste our energy being frustrated.

How we respond to bad news shapes our life for good or bad. But can I let you in on a little secret? The bad news is not our real problem!

There is a great book on how to think called, *As a Man Thinketh*, by James Allen. The book was written back in 1903. This book has had a profound impact on my thinking, second only to the Bible. One of the quotes in this book is, "Circumstances do not make the man; it reveals him to himself." [3] Oh, how we see our true self when we hear bad news! Others know how insecure or worrisome we are because they see how we respond. Or they know we are calm and confident because our character shows itself over and over again. Circumstances are not problems; they are the litmus test that reveals our beliefs.

Another quote, in the same book, really speaks to the power of our thoughts. "The outer world of circumstances shapes itself to the inner world of thought." [4] Let me share a little Fred Talk with you: Think about the power this truth gives you! It makes me think of Jesus when he said, you of little faith, if you have faith as small as a mustard seed, you can say to this mountain move and it will. Nothing will be impossible for you! Be a mountain mover every day, rather than empowering your mountains by thinking your circumstances are too daunting to overcome!

Until we realize that we have complete control over our thoughts and that it's our responsibility to choose what goes in and doesn't go in our mind and heart, we will empower bad news to have a profound effect on our lives. The truth is, bad news only has the power that we give it! If we believe bad news has power, it will, if we don't, it won't. This truth reminds me of another statement from the apostle Paul in Romans 8:28, "*All things work together for good, for those who love the Lord and are called according to his purpose.*" Notice it says ALL things, not some things, not just good things. But if you don't believe that truth, you won't see the fruit of it!

So you might be thinking, how do I know how much influence I give to bad news? How do I figure out what I believe about bad news? It's actually very simple. Just look at your actions. Your actions never lie. It's our interpretation of what we do that isn't always correct. If you get mad easily at bad news or start complaining or give up, then you have your answer! If you really want to know the truth, just ask those closest to you, to be honest, and then see if you get mad at what they tell you! Haha! Now that's funny!

If you're wondering whether bad news has a negative effect on you, then let me suggest to you that you need to do some inner work and settle what you believe about bad news.

You can't be nice with bad news. You can't be kind to negative influences. You must be definitive! You must be in charge of your mind! You are the one who tells yourself what to think about things.

I think we all can say that some of the "worst" experiences in life have turned out to be some of the "best" things for us. They don't always feel like it at first, but if we choose to look for the seed of success in every painful situation, we will find it, because we will learn and grow and become stronger and that will produce something good!

I have chosen to view every difficult and painful experience as something that has a seed of success planted in it. I have decided to forgive myself and others quickly, as fast as it happens, because I've learned that holding onto pain and trying to protect myself or not forgive just causes more pain and does not produce growth or positive fruit.

But Fred, you don't understand what they did to me! No, I don't, but I do understand what unforgiveness does to us.

I am convinced the reason we have a hard time forgiving people is not because of the hurt we've experienced. It's because we are mad and want them to hurt like we did.

We have a belief that forgiveness is letting them off the hook and that they deserve to hurt. If that belief is true God never would have sent his son to die on the cross for us! He didn't let us off the hook, the realities of our own brokenness and sin catch up to us eventually if we don't deal with it. Love doesn't punish for revenge. We only hurt ourselves when we don't forgive.

The Israelites wandered in the desert for 40 years because they chose only to see their pain and view God as unloving and not trustworthy. They would not look for the seed of success in their painful experiences. So they got what they wanted and saw.

Joshua, who 39 years earlier believed that God could help them conquer the promised land that was full of giants looked for a seed of success always, and God rewarded him with the opportunity to lead a new generation of Israelites into the promised land, and they got what they wanted and saw.

Stop blaming your situation, your bad news, that person, or God. You get what you believe and what you want to see.

Remember, my name is Fred, and I'm your friend! Take back the power you keep giving to bad news and other people. Replace your faulty beliefs with the true reality that God loves you and believes in you and that you are strong and courageous no matter what you have to face! You are not alone!

Hearing bad news is one thing. But people who say it the wrong way or when it comes from the wrong person is another issue we have to settle in our hearts. Let me suggest some negative, limiting lies that you might want to replace with life-giving, positive truths!

- My family doesn't know the real me.
- For me to open up, you have to earn my trust.

- Truth only comes from Christians.
- I refuse to learn from people who are mean.
- If you really loved me, you wouldn't say things that hurt me.

There are many more negative, limiting lies we believe about others that produces the very thing we believe. Re-read each of those statements and grasp the gravity of what you are creating each time you think and believe those thoughts about others.

Now look at how replacing those thoughts with positive, life-giving truths creates good fruit.

- My family loves me and believes in me and celebrates my strengths.
- I am open with people and choose to trust the best in others and believe people rise to what you expect of them.
- When people don't live up to what they say, we talk openly about it and create a plan to move them to greater responsibility.
- I learn from everyone; truth comes in all types of experiences. I sift what is true and not true from all the interactions I have.
- People often are afraid or hurt and say things to protect themselves; I choose not to believe those things and know that I am loved no matter what people say. My strength will help others heal from their brokenness and find hope.

Get the picture? Spend some time identifying negative, limiting beliefs that you have so you can replace them with positive, life-giving truths.

A word about doctors: I have a tremendous amount of respect for doctors and am very thankful to my surgeon and oncology doctors who were used by God to help remove my cancer and teach me about how our bodies work.

Jesus is referred to in scripture as our great physician; people who devote the time to study our bodies design and serve others by working to provide healing are in a noble profession. I have met many leading doctors who humbly acknowledge God's sovereign knowledge and power over their life.

So thank your doctors for their service! But NEVER give up your belief that God is the one who is in control of your life and that you have the power to speak life into any situation you face!

We are subconsciously trained at a very young age that certain professionals know best: doctors, financial advisors, and educators. Never give away your authority on your life to someone else. We tell ourselves we're not smart enough to know if something is wrong in our body and we have to go to a doctor to be healed or take some pill. We tell ourselves we don't know the best way to invest our money and just give it to someone else and hope they know best. We assume because someone is smart and has a doctorate at a college that they understand life more than we do.

I'm not saying don't go to doctors, or don't use financial advisors or get an education. I'm saying, don't allow yourself to believe the lie that your hope is in someone else. God created you in His image; He has unlimited potential and is the whole reason you are breathing right now! You have the ability to think and create just like God. You have access to his supernatural knowledge about the laws of nature that when put into practice, can self-heal and enable you to grow your business or wealth and gain invaluable insight into life and people.

I've had many breakthroughs in my life that came from within. God said, we are the temple of the living God, his spirit is in us. He helps us discern and know what to do or say.

I used to have to take allergy shots and antibiotics constantly. I used to have major lower back issues that limited me and caused tremendous pain. I used to not know anything about business and now run multiple successful businesses. I used to live paycheck to paycheck and now know how to reinvest to produce more income even when I'm not working. I have a lot more to say about these truths, but just know this; you have everything in you that you need to become the person God made you to be! Believe that and grow your faith muscle in God and yourself, and you will see the fruit of it!

BREAKING THE NEWS

I took Dyan to dinner the night of my doctor's appointment. I wanted the news to be shared in the context of a special night out together! We enjoyed our meal and laughed and talked for a while; then after we finished eating, I told her I had something I needed to tell her. She immediately knew that it was something serious. I reached across the table and grabbed her hands and said, "Do you remember when I took Seth to the doctor to get his warts frozen off, and they cut a mole off on my knee?" She said, "Yes." "Well, the doctor called me at the end of last week and told me it was Malignant Melanoma Skin Cancer. She told me I would have to have surgery because it was deeper than they cut. I didn't say anything at first because it was Homecoming weekend and I didn't have any answers, and I wanted Chelsea and you to be able to enjoy the weekend. I met with the doctor today, and he shared everything with me so that I could explain things to you and the kids."

At first, Dyan was shocked and then shared how she was so sorry I went through this week alone, and she would have wanted to be there. I reassured her that I was okay and just wanted to be able to know what was going on before sharing, so it was most helpful for our family.

Then she broke into 20 questions. She fired off one after another, and I was able to answer all but one. The only question she had that I didn't have an answer to was, "Is it anywhere else in your body?" That one we would have to find out as we progressed with the surgery.

Her first question was, "When is the surgery." She grasped the gravity of how serious this was. I told her that there were two options when I called: the following week or three weeks from now. I explained that I had chosen the later surgery due to a trip to Africa we had on the calendar to visit our orphan care ministry team that our church-sponsored, and I was coaching my son's little league football championship game.

She abruptly said, "You are calling the nurse back first thing tomorrow morning and changing it to the earlier time if it's still available. We are not waiting and letting it grow more. We will cancel our Africa trip and go another time, and someone else can coach the game!" Can you hear Mama Bear? Well, I listened wisely to the Holy Spirit, challenging my views! Husbands, you do know that God often speaks through our wives, don't you? The next morning I called and was able to move my surgery up to the following week.

After we spent about an hour at the restaurant talking through our new reality of cancer, our next step was to share with our kids. We briefly discussed our approach, and both agreed that we needed to let them know and that we would choose to use this as a teaching opportunity to show them how to demonstrate your positive faith in God no matter what you face. We've learned over the years that the best way to grow your personal faith is to face tough realities head-on and believe God is with you, loves you, and will guide you through it! Jesus said nothing is impossible with God. Live like you believe it!

So we went home and gathered our kids in the living room. Chelsea was 15, Seth was 13, and Luke was 8. Our youngest wasn't worried about it; I'm not sure he really grasped what cancer even is. He was off playing as soon as we shared. Our older kids were at a very impressionable age as teenagers and understood the reality that cancer means you could lose your dad. They had more questions, and even though they didn't talk a lot about it, we knew they were thinking about it because they would have random questions from time to time that were pretty deep.

We explained everything we knew and then reassured our kids we believed God had allowed us to catch this early enough to remove it and that I was going to be okay. Then we prayed together and hugged! I asked each of my kids recently about that day. Now that they are older, they all said they were afraid, but believed I was going to be okay.

Let me take a moment and share some parenting advice here. Dyan and I have always used the approach, that if we are going to share with the kids about something difficult we are facing, we need to first be on the same page together. If we are struggling with it, then we wait because it's not our kid's responsibility to struggle with our issues. This way of parenting has saved our kids from having to work through a lot of baggage that is not theirs. We practiced this principle of only sharing what we we're united on.

When it came to the times when we were not getting along as a couple, when we had relational issues at the church we pastored, or when we had extended family issues, we always felt our kids didn't need to know our crap unless we could share it without dumping it on them.

We now see the benefit of this approach as they are older. We've had some talks about issues that they wondered about, that now as adults, they see the full picture but are thankful we didn't bring them into it at the time. Our kids have a close relationship with both of us, they have a very positive image of the church and people in general, they feel safe to be themselves around us, and they trust our advice when they share with us about their own issues. We feel very blessed as parents!

So don't let scary news and difficult situations influence your family negatively. Be strong and courageous in how to approach things together!

One of my favorite characters in the Bible is Joshua. He's the one who God chose to lead the Israelites into the Promised Land. He took all kinds of new territory for God's people. In fact, God said he had already given him everywhere he was going to step foot. Then

God told him I am with you, so be strong and courageous, rather than afraid and discouraged. I have told myself that truth over and over again in most situations I face. God has already given me where I am stepping foot today, and He is with me, go take new ground with confidence! I hope you are beginning to see that you can face anything with strength and courage because it's all about mindset! Once you get that right, the rest takes care of itself!

Lead your family out of a place of security that you are not alone! Walk humbly with your God, and you will help others around you experience the reality of God's presence. They may not realize what it is you have, but over time, people will see a depth of character and peace that shows them the true God. When you live out of this truth, it infects others with positivity, hope, and love. This is how God is honored, when you show others his character through your daily life! So no matter what you face, do it with grace!

SPECIAL CONNECTION

There is something special about going through cancer. You have an instant bond with others who have experienced the battle. People you've never met feel close to you and open up immediately. I've had whole families share with me about their experiences with a family member once they found out about my cancer background. I would liken it to war veterans or teams who went through a difficult season and came out champions. There is something about the spirit of overcoming that links us with one another!

There were two very special connections I had during my cancer, and both of them came within the first week! The first was my sister-in-law Suzi. From the moment I met Suzi, we were always close. I can remember the first time we met. I was waiting in the lobby of Dyan's dorm; it was Homecoming weekend, so Woogs (that's Suzi's nickname from growing up) came to visit her sister. She walked into the lobby, and immediately yelled "Freddy!" and came and gave me a big hug! Suzi was a former cheerleader and always positive and full of life! Then she stopped for a second and said, "You are Freddy, right?" We both laughed!

Suzi had gone through breast cancer seven years earlier. She had a mastectomy. She had been doing great! She would go to her annual checkups and always got a good report. The week after I was diagnosed, Suzi found out that her cancer had come back in the same spot. My wife had to hear from her sister and husband within a week that they both had cancer. As soon as Suzi found out about her cancer, she called me. It was like we were instantly bonded on a whole new level!

Suzi is also a nurse, so anytime someone in the family is sick; we call the "family physician." Suzi had her 20 questions for me from a medical viewpoint. She wanted to know how deep the cancer was in millimeters; she wanted to know about my surgeon and what the treatment plan was. Then after the medical questions, we talked about the deeper questions of how we were feeling. Throughout the course of our procedures and treatments, we would call each other to check-in.

I remember on my way to my first surgery I told Dyan I felt like I needed to call Woogs. Dyan wanted to get to be with me since I was about to go under the knife, but I remember feeling this sense that I needed to encourage her. And sure enough, when Suzi answered she was struggling with some fear about this being the second time around and being a very aggressive form of cancer.

We talked, and I was able to reassure her of God's protection and healing on her life, then I hung up and felt ready to face my procedure. Dyan thanked me for supporting her sister and was impressed with how I was able to be focused on helping Suzi while I was on my way to my own surgery. The only way I can explain it is, I didn't think it was my time to go, I still sensed that God had a lot more he wanted me to do, so I wasn't worried and believed He was going to use my cancer to help a lot of people, so I didn't need to be afraid. That sense of peace freed me to focus my attention on others.

Suzi and I had a special connection that was always intuitive. There were numerous times where we would call and encourage each other. Our struggles were different. Suzi was dealing with having to go back through the same struggle, but with an even more aggressive form of cancer, so her fear was related to why again and can she beat it again? Suzi had panic attacks that would come on her, and she would be paralyzed with fear, where nothing rational would help relieve the feeling.

Later on, I would experience panic attacks when recovering from my treatment, and they were very scary. I learned that when someone is emotionally hurt or scared, logic doesn't help! Physically being present and emotionally connecting with someone is what helps!

I have to admit for most of my marriage, I've done a lousy job of coming alongside my wife on an emotional level when she just needs to share how she's feeling. I like to fix things like a typical guy. So I go into logic and answers, this never helps! I now understand why!

It reminds me of the scripture that says mourn with those who mourn, weep with those who weep. Entering into someone's pain and loving them through it is not easy. It takes a lot of courage and strength. My wife has a doctorate in this as you will find out in a later chapter.

There were times when I was recovering from my depression that was caused by the drug I took that Suzi would call me and give me a stern pep talk about needing to find a job to provide for my family and not wallow in my self-pity. We could talk very frankly with each other since we both could say; I know what you are going through! We also were able to celebrate with each other each time we had good reports and hit new milestones of one year, two years, and five years out! Suzi also whipped her cancer!

I remember the day I told Suzi that the doctor said he didn't need to see me anymore! No more ex-rays! We both celebrated at a deep soul level because we knew what each other was going through! I still see my oncologist and my dermatologist once a year. Suzi also has annual checkups. We are both very thankful and feel that God has been very good to us!

The other special connection I had was with a young boy who was going through bone marrow cancer. His name is Trevor Cobb, and he loves football! He is a twin, and his brother was on my son's team! As soon as I heard my news I talked with Trev about his journey with cancer, and he had been through multiple surgeries and treatments, and he was not able to play his favorite sport due to his bone cancer that was in his leg. We immediately become buddies!

As I learned about his journey, I was so impressed with his courage and toughness as an eight-year-old! His parents did everything they could to support their son, endless nights at the hospitals, traveling all around the country for the best treatments, walking through each day with Trevor as he battled over and over again for years! We had many Saturdays at games where we would high five each other and check-in with each other! Trevor is now 16 and a healthy teenage athlete!

I also got pretty close to my cancer team! My oncologist Dr. Bhatia told me, "You don't want to see me! If you have to see me, it's not good!" We laugh about that at my annual checkups. I also developed a special relationship with Trisha Yoder, my doctor's assistant. She had such a kind spirit, and after checking me over would sit back and smile and say, "How are you doing?" When I went through my depression due to the medication, she was a big encourager, and as I started to finally pull out of my depression after a year and a half I remember the day she said to me, "You look really good!" I told her I felt really good! Trisha was pregnant with twins when I was going through my treatments, so we would often talk about how her kids are doing now!

Then there was Brenda Fernandes, the secretary. Each time I would check in she was always so positive. She would tell me, "You're so young to be battling cancer!" Each year I come for my checkups she sees me, and we both get a really big smile and hug! She sees a lot of heartache and loss with families, so there is something special about being able to see someone make it through!

Then there are all of the people I meet and families who are touched by cancer. I am grateful that God allowed me to go through cancer so I can connect with people who are struggling and need some encouragement! People just open up and feel so safe to talk as soon as they hear I'm a cancer survivor. I count that as a privilege to minister to people uniquely because of my personal experience! What a gift! I thank the good Lord every day to be used in this way!

I believe one of the reasons God allows us to go through some of the challenges we face is to encourage others. The scriptures talk about the hope we are able to offer others because of the struggles we have faced.

I wouldn't wish cancer on anyone, but I'm good with the fact that God allowed me to go through what I went through, in fact, I'm even okay if God planned it and gave it to me! How can I say that? Why can we only give God credit for planning the things we view as good? Many people are quick to say that God guided me and blessed me with my job or my spouse or my kids or …

Cancer has changed me in a very good way and put me on a path that I would never have chosen, and I am very grateful for that! Even the low places I went with depression have sensitized me to a world that I didn't even know existed that now I can speak into to help others know there is hope!

The apostle Paul talks about how he grew to thank God for his trials. I understand his mindset now! In all things, whether they look good or bad, thank the Lord! Because God is good! He is loving! Even if it doesn't look or feel like it. He's a really, really good Dad!

I trust my Heavenly Father even when it's hard because I know his heart is pure. There is no reason for me to doubt his love or goodness just because my life is painful. I know that he will use everything for his good and my good! And I don't have to wait until I understand it to know this truth or thank him!

And this truth has helped me understand a secret! It's a secret that anyone can learn, but many people don't ever understand because of a mindset that limits their view of God. None of us enjoys pain for pain's sake. But I have learned that any pain we are going through will last longer if we choose to fight it. We end up wallowing in the wilderness like the Israelites did that chose not to trust God's heart! They ended up getting what they feared and projected on God.

But if we will learn to always look for the seed of success in every painful situation, not only will the pain last shorter, we won't spend much time lost in the wilderness. When you are looking for the good in a situation, you find it. You are teachable; you learn lessons quickly and change your mindset and actions follow. When you have a trusting heart, you see and hear God clearly! And people are attracted to you because you are resilient and hopeful.

So if you want special connections and want your life to impact others every day, choose to believe there is a seed of success in every painful experience you face!

Look for the seed of success, so you have a growth mindset, own what you can, forgive yourself and others quickly, so you're focus can stay positive, and you will magically see what others can't see! You will have a grounded confidence that others will want! You will find victory and success and fulfillment in your relationships and life work!

HANDLING EVERYONE ELSE'S FEARS

After sharing with Dyan and the kids, we then told our parents and siblings, church family and friends. The response was the same every time, shock, and immediately put me on the prayer chain at their churches! My parents and Dyan's mom immediately put us on every prayer chain in the nation! I had thousands of people, some I knew, and most I didn't praying for me! People would reply to my blogs that I didn't know; I experienced the power of people's prayers!

One of my dearest friends for over 20 years, who I had the privilege of leading to Christ and baptizing in the first month of our church plant, is Shane Foley. When I met Shane, he didn't like church, but he connected with our approach. So we became fast friends.

I needed someone to take me to a couple of oncology appointments so we could decide which doctor and hospital we wanted to use. Shane volunteered to drive me. When we got to the cancer center he went to drop me off, and I said, no I need you to go in so you can help write things down also. Dyan couldn't go because of her new job as a school counselor, so we wanted a second set of ears. Shane was mortified! He planned to stay as far away from the doctor and news as he could. Later we laughed about how he was scared to death to hear someone tell him that his friend and pastor was probably going to die of cancer! Shane was a real trooper!

A lot of people don't like to talk about death. They hate funeral homes and get the heebie-jeebies! That's when you feel like you're going to throw up and want to get out of there.

I grew up around death, hospitals, and funeral homes since my dad was a pastor. I went to see people sick and was there when many people died. I always had confidence in God and knew that life is way bigger than just the physical things we see! I know there is eternal life. I know if you put your faith in Jesus Christ, things will be okay, because it's not something we have to try to earn. So when it comes to dealing with people's fears about death and life, I'm very comfortable talking about those things!

I remember my Dad saying; "You would be the last person I would expect to have cancer because of how well you take care of your body working out and eating. It doesn't seem fair." The medical community is not sure what exactly causes melanoma skin cancer. There is a belief that sunburns are a primary cause, but it's not like I ever got sun-burned behind my knee. And I didn't burn any more than the average kid. It doesn't seem fair. If there is one thing I would suggest never to spend time contemplating in life, it would be that statement. It's not fair!

Whenever I have allowed myself to believe that something is unfair, it never goes anywhere good! That statement puts us in a defensive, revengeful mindset. It also pits us against God and makes it almost impossible to view our Creator as a loving heavenly Father who cares about us.

I know that sometimes we are wronged in life, and trust me; I've had my fair share of it. But winning that battle leaves us prideful and selfish. Think about it, what is fair? It's what we want; it's what makes us right; it's totally subjective. We all tend to agree in society that no one is perfect, so then how can we even begin to go down the rabbit trail of comparing ourselves to others or what is fair? We don't truly want what is fair! Even the best of us in our worst moments have done something we are ashamed of and are tremendously thankful for forgiveness.

Most people think life isn't fair, and it's not my fault! Let me ask you to consider one question if that's what you believe, how's that belief working out for you? The quicker we own our part and realize that we're stuck on the wrong belief, the better. NEVER focus on what life is NOT! That is negative energy that will only produce negative results.

Pastors and Christians are often quick to say that the Bible doesn't say that life will be fair, that God never promised that life would be easy as if fair means easy. There is no growth without challenges, so it's not unfair that life has challenges. We tend to view our circumstances in a vacuum, how could they cut me off like that, yet we've made driving mistakes also. I didn't deserve for them to dump on me, yet we've dumped on people before.

The Bible actually teaches that God IS fair. He is just. Jesus said good people produce good fruit; bad people produce bad fruit. The Bible also teaches that we shouldn't be deceived, God is not mocked, whatever a man sows, he reaps. I could go on and share lots of other scriptures that talk about how life is fair, and how God designed the world to function by these laws.

Before I go any further, let me first say, God's heart breaks when people are treated unjustly. Men will pay for raping women. Those who steal and don't make amends will pay for what they took. And there are painful things that happen to us that we don't always create, like losing a child or a spouse. We all have painful experiences and losses that hurt. But how we choose to view our pain determines the direction our life takes. So our beliefs shape our lives for good or bad! So please allow me to push us a little on what we really believe. Remember, my name is Fred, and I'm your friend!

It's in times of personal pain when we wrestle with questions like why do bad things happen to good people. That is a very loaded question! First off, what constitutes bad? Some of the worst things in my life that have happened to me have turned out to be the best things! The God of the universe, who is perfect and created everything and everyone for the purpose of life together, was rejected by his own creation (you and me) over and over again in every generation until He eventually chose to sacrifice His own son to save us from our sinful nature that hurts people.

God didn't cry foul and choose to blame us and demand justice; instead, He accepted pain and lovingly provided a way to restore humanity. Why? Because He believes we were worth it!

So who's good? The Bible says that only God is good! I would highly recommend you settle this one as quickly as you can in your heart and mind that God is the only one who is fair and we don't deserve anything. So be thankful for whatever you have and live life with open hands receiving whatever blessings God grants us and letting go of whatever we think we deserve so we can manage losses and hurts with grace. I'm not better than anyone else, so it doesn't help for me to claim life is not fair, like I'm good.

I believe that we get what we chase after in life. God designed nature to run by the laws of cause and effect. Positive causes produce positive effects. Negative causes produce negative effects. If you evaluate most of life, you will begin to see that our world pretty much gives us what we deserve. Work hard, treat people with respect, do the right thing, and life goes well. Violate those principles and reap the negative consequences as a result. Think about your relationships, work, finances, health, and you will see that for the most part, life gives us what we choose. If we manage our money well, we do okay. If we spend more than we make life is frustrating. If we eat well and stay active, we feel good if we are not disciplined in those areas we struggle.

Life is run by law, not chaos and disorder. This is how God designed things to be. Most of life is orderly. We drive on our side of the road and the overwhelming majority of the time we go where we want to and so do millions of other people. So if life on a large scale is generally fair, then why do so many of us tend to struggle with life not being fair? I propose that it's because we have a belief system that makes us feel like a victim and doubt the goodness of God and others. For example:

- loss is bad
- life should be easy
- I'm a good person
  (better than people who hurt me)
- pain is bad

If I believe these things, then when those things happen, the assumption is that life is not fair. But it's more about our mindset than it is about what happens.

I run a few businesses. One is a painting business. Sometimes clients can be very difficult and cruel in what they say about our employees. It's very easy to view this as unfair and vilify people and play the victim. But in reality, we all can be difficult and cruel at times. There are many reasons people respond negatively. I'm not trying to dismiss behavior, it's just a part of life, and it helps us grow and learn how to navigate people and sometimes speak life and hope into others who desperately need it!

Let me say it a little clearer. Grow up! Remember, my name is Fred, and I'm your friend! True friends say what we need to hear and call us to more. Growth and character require challenges and pain and stretching. This is good and fair! Accept it and enjoy life and people no matter what you face or don't and fight and complain about your life.

If we want health, we tend to get it because we do the things that produce good health. If we want loving relationships, we tend to get them because we focus on love. If we want achievements, we tend to get them because we focus on the things that create success. If we want to honor God with our life, we tend to make decisions that grow strong character and influence others positively. These are all good things that we should aspire to. But as we move in these directions we have situations and people we have to navigate along the way that are challenging, or we didn't see coming.

Our greatest pain in life comes from becoming so attached to things, needing them so much that we try to control them and can't let go. Growth by nature requires change. If I want to get stronger, I have to let go of comfort and control and push myself. If I want to develop, I can't worry so much about what others think of me and must be willing to move onto new life-giving relationships.

Instead of asking, why did that happen to me? Why did they say that about me? Try asking a different question: "Why NOT ME?" Maybe God is trying to grow you and change you so you will quit staying stuck and attached to things and people. When people would say to me, "Why did you get cancer?" I would say back, "Why not me?!?" "Why me" questions NEVER lead to growth! A why not me attitude positions us in a growth mode! So when you have bad news, remember, it's all about how you view it! Position yourself and others for growth!

If you haven't picked this up yet in life, I'll let you in on a little secret. Most people live their lives in fear. They don't realize it, but most of what we do is driven by fear.

People stay in jobs that are not fulfilling or healthy environments for fear of not having money to provide. People let others talk to them rudely and take advantage of them then only complain to their friends about it for fear of standing up to someone and making them mad or not like you. People don't talk about their faith for fear of losing their job. People don't share their real feelings for fear that they will be rejected. People are indecisive because they don't want to make a mistake. I could go on and on.

Of course, you don't live your life in fear! At least, that's what we tell ourselves. Because we are afraid to take a deep, honest look at our life and ask the tough questions:

- Why am I not fulfilled in my relationships and work?

- Why am I not doing what I really feel led to do?

- Why do I always feel like I don't know what to say to people when they share challenges with me?

See, unless you become aware that most people live by fear and make decisions from fear you will just go through life listening to all of the negative, fearful talk from others and it will influence you without even knowing it.

I talked about the energy our thoughts put out and how it shapes our actions and life. Animals know this truth also. They can sense fear in a human immediately. They pick up on the vibes we put off. And they go on the attack. But if they sense a human that is strong and confident, they will be submissive.

Our talk gives away what drives our life. If we are always doubting, questioning, hesitant, talking about the problems, those are all negative vibes that we emit to others. When you become aware that our thoughts and words have life or death in them, you begin to realize that you have to guard your mind. You are in charge of what goes in!

The Bible spends a lot of time talking about mindset; how you think. Because God knows our thoughts shape our lives. Scripture teaches that we are to put on the full armor of God. Every day we go to battle, the first piece of armor we are supposed to wear is the helmet of salvation. A helmet protects your brain;

it keeps negative thoughts out! When you understand what God did for you on the cross through his son Jesus Christ, you know that he saved you, so you are now viewed as holy in God's eyes. You are a new creation. So guard your mind and don't let negative self-talk in. God loves you, forgives you, and believes in you! Think about those things that are true and positive and good. Choose to live your life from a place of security and confidence. Make your decisions from courage, not fear.

Hardships test us and either grow our character or make us shrink back. Choose who you want to be and chase after it with all you have and don't let other people's negative thoughts and opinions in your mind.

WHY ME?

People who need to know all the answers spend most of their life self-absorbed. I'm not sure why I got cancer. But I have some strong hunches. The more important question to answer is what can I learn from getting cancer, and how can I use it to grow stronger? When we focus on growth and strength, we are guaranteed to be able to face anything in life and create positive results from it, because our vibrations of energy are moving in a productive pattern and that attracts more of the same! When our thoughts are oriented in a life-giving direction, we see what we are looking for and therefore create opportunities that others don't see.

I choose life, I choose positivity, I choose hope, I choose love, I choose victory. These are all truths that God has already planned for our lives, but we must do our part of believing them about our life. Faith is not some theory we believe; it is something that propels us to action forward in spite of what we see or don't see. There is no faith or belief without action. If you say you believe something and don't live it, you don't believe it. It's just that simple! So quit kidding yourself! Scripture says that fools say they believe something but don't actually do what they say. Remember, my name is Fred, and I'm your friend!

I believe the reason most of us struggle with what we believe is because we don't know God. We have heard things about Him and read about Him in the Bible, but we haven't experienced the power of who

He really is. So before I give God credit for my cancer, let me help you understand why I'm okay with that! Let me help you get to know the ONE and ONLY TRUE LIVING GOD!

Let's start with our little science lesson again. We all know that our universe is constantly expanding. The technology we have developed has allowed us to realize that our little world and even our galaxy are not the largest things on the block! Our universe is growing at the speed of light getting larger as we speak. So we could say it's limitless! There is no end in sight! The Sun, which is massive and powers all life on Earth from millions of miles away, is one of the smaller stars in the universe. So what we can actually see and know blows our mind away!

So let's consider the source of all of this massive limitless live-giving universe. Where does all that power and growth come from? It's Creator! Intelligent life comes from an intelligent creator. Computers are not made by a random chance of spontaneous combustion. An intelligent creator who has a specific purpose in mind for the use of the device builds it with painstaking detail. The Bible teaches that before the world we see even existed the eternal God has always been and always will be. He stretches out the heavens and gives life to everything; all of nature's laws are empowered by Him! The reason God is referred to as the Lord is because he is the source of everything and has complete control and authority over every form of life.

And this eternal, limitless, all-powerful God says that you and I are his crowning achievement! This God is where love comes from. He intentionally decided to create humans in His image so He could share His love and truth with us! Then He gave us the freedom to choose what we want from life. No other life form gets that privilege of choice. Animals, plants, earth, our solar systems, they all exist to serve and worship their Creator. But we get to choose.

There is evidence everywhere we turn of a loving and holy creator, yet scripture teaches the very first humans chose to reject God and wanted to be their own god. Every generation and person that has ever lived does the same thing. Can you imagine as a parent, the pain God must feel? He just wants to love and bless us and guide us to all of His glorious truths and share life with us, but we're too busy, we're too smart, we blame Him, we demand our way!

And what did our perfect Heavenly Father do? He decided to become a human, Jesus Christ, and make a way for us to find our way back to Him! He subjected himself to his own creation to demonstrate His immense love and loyalty to us! He ended up dying for us, so our sins of rebellion could be dealt with. Justice demands a price to be paid for choices.

When we choose truth and love, we receive eternal life and blessings! When we choose to reject the truth and go our own way, we receive eternal separation and punishment. It's our choice! But there are real consequences to our choices. I find it interesting that people are so quick to want justice when they are wronged but then can struggle with a perfect and holy Creator, who is incredibly patient with His creation, having clear boundaries with consequences. The gift of choice brings with it responsibilities. We get to choose our destiny!

People often struggle with the idea of knowing God, but He has clearly shown who He is to us and relates to us in the same way we relate to others. We have a mind, body, and spirit. We were created in the image of God. God the Father (Mind/Creator), the Son (body), and the Holy Spirit (power). People often struggle with the idea of the Trinity, but it's very simple! I am 3 persons in one. I am a Father, Son, and Husband. I relate completely differently and am seen differently to those people, but I am one person.

God, the creator, decided to create a world for us humans so he could share his love and truth with us. He spoke everything into existence with his word, which was Christ, and then his word became flesh, Jesus. We got to see a real tangible fleshly example of God in human form. He died for us as a perfect sacrifice, took our sins on himself willingly to pay the price that was due to justice, showing us how much he loves us. Then He defeated death and the Prince of Darkness and is now seated on the right hand of God on the Throne in Heaven. Then God sent his Holy Spirit to live in us and empower us to become the men and women he made us to be. He speaks to our hearts and works among us. The Bible is God's recorded words to us so we could get to know him. So get to know the REAL God!

If God is everywhere and all-powerful and easy to get to know, then why is it so hard for us to believe in miraculous stories from history and scripture that talk about incredible things God does? Why do we worry about our own basic needs of life? Why do we feel so powerless to our circumstances? Because you don't know the ONE and ONLY TRUE LIVING GOD! Remember, my name is Fred, and I'm your friend! When we were little kids, and a bully came up to us, we could say my Dad will beat you up! We knew our Dad could take anyone and would defend us! Because he loved us! We were his!

Our Heavenly Father is infinitely more powerful than Arnold Schwarzenegger and the Hulk and more loving than Mother Teresa. If you really believe God loves you and He is who He says He is, then you're good! You don't have to fear what will happen when you die; you don't have to prove anything, you don't have to spend a single second questioning anything you face, no matter how painful or scary. Because God is with you and He is in control. He made everything, so He's more than capable of working things out for you!

We're so impressed with our ability to create technology and gain knowledge. But we are only able to create from what is already here. God created what we create with! He designed every single one of your millions of nerve cells in your brain so you could think logically. So, from this place of truth, we can live our lives with confidence! Quit wasting time on questions and doubts and start living your life with purpose and power!

Now that you know the REAL GOD let me share with you why I think I got cancer. Maybe my views won't be quite as scary for you to hear now!

The first reason I believe I got cancer was because God planned it, He wanted to use my life to touch millions of people who live in fear and limited thoughts about themselves and God to help those people unlock their full God-given potential. Fear and limiting thoughts hold us back from becoming the person God made us to be, and from producing the results we want relationally and professionally.

Most of us are not aware that we live in fear and limiting thoughts, so God puts people in our lives to help us become aware of these negative influences so we can identify them, remove them and replace them with positive, life-giving beliefs about ourselves, God and others!

When we see someone else deal with fears and limiting thoughts and overcome, it gives us a picture, a vision of hope that can propel us toward a new life! When someone overcomes difficult circumstances, it takes positive thoughts and energy. Those positive vibrations of energy are felt when we hear someone share, and it influences us. We can sense a spirit of strength that comes from a life that has been tested, and it infects our spirit in a positive way.

The Bible says that faith comes from hearing. I talked earlier about how our thoughts are vibrations of energy. Sound waves are vibrations of energy. The vibe we put off with our words and actions either produces faith or fear. Most of us don't realize that we are putting off a vibe of fear with all of our questions and doubts and hesitation. But once we hear the story of someone who has dealt with the same things we have and overcame it and is thriving, it makes us aware of just how negative our frequency is.

I count it a privilege that God would choose to use my life to impact others positively; that He would entrust me with the opportunity to speak into others lives and inspire them to dream big and let go of their fears and limitations so they can become the men and women He made them to be!

I believe God chose to use cancer as one of those means to this end. He also used depression and a career change in my mid 40's that was a huge pay cut while I had kids in college. I could wallow in self-pity about those challenges (which I did for over a year and wasted a lot of time and caused my wife a lot of heartache), or I can welcome struggles as opportunities to help everyone else who deals with scary health or mental issues and financial setbacks and work insecurities.

Why has the STRONG movement been such a huge success with cancer patients and families? Because when we see people overcome negative, fearful, difficult situations, it gives us hope that we can too! The vibrations of energy the STRONG movement puts off breathes life and hope into us! Everyone is touched by cancer. We all have family and friends who are impacted by it. I believe God uses these types of movements to breathe hope and life into humanity, whether people give God the credit for it or not.

And here's another truth I have learned that may be hard to hear! So please remember, my name is Fred, and I'm your friend! If we view our health issue as a curse or unfortunate card we were dealt, then that's all we will ever get out of it. The power of a positive attitude, choosing to see setbacks as a blessing or seed for success is the key to physical and mental recovery and making our life count for good with others! I'm not saying every health issue will be fully resolved, but I know for a fact that if we view it positively we will be healthier and it's our primary healing agent, even more than doctors and medicine.

Studies have been done about the power of positive thinking and prayer on healing. God is the source of all healing, whether it is through a doctor, medication, or our beliefs. Please hear me on this friend; we have way more power to self-heal that we realize! Later on in the chapter when I talk about my battle with depression, you will hear me affirm that I needed medication to balance out my levels and help me get on a level playing field emotionally. So I'm not saying there is not a place for medication and doctors. But I also came to a place where I knew it was time to get off of medicine and I was afraid. That fear told me I was putting my hope in a pill rather than in my Creator and myself. I was reminded of the scripture that teaches not to let anything control you.

I believe we have an internal sense of truth that helps us know the right thing to do. I'm not talking about a feel-good theology that is totally subjective. Truth does not reside in us. Truth is universal and comes from an eternal source. But the scriptures teach that God has placed this eternal truth in us. And it always lines up with what God teaches in scripture. This is why memorization of God's word is so helpful; it allows us to draw from truth quickly so we can make wise decisions. I'll talk more in a later chapter about how memorizing scriptures helped me overcome depression. But even without scripture, God has placed in every person in every nation a conscience that knows certain things are wrong, but we often deceive ourselves into thinking what I want is good and right. God corrects us through his Holy Spirit that convicts us; He also uses consequences and people.

Jesus healed a lot of people when he was on the Earth, and he didn't perform one surgery or give any medications unless you count mud and spit, which He used to help blind men see! I just think that's hilarious! The God of the universe put mud on a blind guy's eyes and then had him wash it off with water, and he was healed and could see! Another time Jesus spat in a man's eyes and healed his sight. Can you imagine going to a medical professional and they use mud or spit on you to heal you! Come on people, that's just really funny! What was God trying to teach us by doing that? Let's not get over spiritual and say Jesus' spit made the mud become some special holy muddy water!

Remember, God made everything; He knows all of the elements in dirt and water. In fact, I think he was taking people back to how humanity was created; the Bible teaches that God took dust and breathed life into it to create the first man. That's why scripture also says we return to the dust when we die.

So here's the principle I'm getting at. Healing comes first from God! For centuries people have been looking for healing from everything else first. We try medical remedies, doctors, books… Jesus healed a woman who had been bleeding for twelve years, people who had been lame for thirty years, one little girl was dying and had suffered greatly at the hand of many doctors and just gotten worse, then Jesus comes and heals them. And he would always say, you're faith has healed you!

I know there is a lot of negativity around faith healing, many people have been told they did not have enough faith, and that is why a loved one did not get better. Jesus did tell his followers a few times they needed to stop doubting, but then he healed people. He didn't leave people feeling disempowered. He actually said if you just have faith as small as a mustard seed you can say to a mountain move and it will move! He spoke in ways that grew people's faith. He helped people realize that they had small views of

God that were limiting them, and replaced their fears and limiting views with pictures of hope and strength. He always asked people, "What do you want?"

Your faith has healed you! What an empowering statement! Let's go back to a truth I shared earlier; we create our destiny by our thoughts. Everything starts in your mind. Everything we see was once a vision in someone's mind that they chose to then act on and create it. Jesus was teaching people how to bring about healing in their own lives. It all starts in our mind! What do you believe? What do you want?

As soon as I ask that question the doubters jump in with their sound reasoning and say, but you don't want to get your hopes up, you need to be realistic. Just listen to how negative and disempowering that statement is. When did God ever do anything realistic? What's wrong with getting your hopes up, having a positive attitude? I understand what people are saying, I've tried it, and it didn't work, and it hurt! So I'm not putting myself through that again! WOW! Just listen to the future someone is sealing for themselves with those words!

Friends, I've believed for some really BIG things and fallen flat on my face! But that doesn't mean it doesn't work, that doesn't mean God didn't care, that doesn't mean I should give up! That type of reasoning is a lie, and it cripples us in fear and limits our view of God and our own potential. I've evaluated my times when things didn't work out, and here's what I've learned, blaming and closing off never helps. I can give you a dozen reasons why things didn't turn out, and I've learned that it's very short-sighted of me to conclude that God didn't care or wasn't strong enough.

I'm not God, so I don't understand the scope of humanity as he does. The scriptures say we can see only a reflection as, in a mirror, we only know in part, but will one day see in full. God allows us to see enough to know He is loving and just and all-powerful. But just as when we were kids, we didn't always understand why our parents didn't do what we wanted them to do. All I know is that the kind of faith that works trusts that God knows best and is always acting out of love, even if it is painful for me right now! I have settled that one in my heart because I don't want to be double-minded.

As your friend, let me speak into your life and relationships by suggesting that we are creating a lot of our own pain and disconnect by what we believe about those we say we love.

- You never…
- If you would just …
- Why don't you …

The statements we tell ourselves and those closest to us shape our results!

Here's a truth you can build your life on friends! Until you start believing and speaking positive statements about your life backed with definitive emotions, you will always be wishing life were different!

Life is what you make it, so what do you want? Tell yourself and others that you already have it then! The scriptures say, "As a man thinketh, so he is." We tell ourselves what to do, and our body is servant to the mind. Quit trying and saying what you wish were different. Believe your life is worth something and that the people you love are worth something and act out of that truth. Life doesn't give you what you wish for. It gives you what you create. You create what you believe! My friend, you have way more power inside of you than you realize!

God said that with Him, ALL things are possible. In fact, even without God, incredible things are possible! There's a story in the Old Testament of the Tower of Babel, where people decided to build a city and a tower that reaches to the heavens so that they could make a name for themselves. And you know what God said about that? As one people speaking the same language, nothing they plan to do will be impossible for them. So God confused their language so they couldn't understand each other.

God knows the power we have to create our life when we come together as one, whether it's for good or bad. We do a lot of creating that is not good. And I'm talking about you and me, not all the other people in the world who are so bad.

We ruin our own marriages, pass on our own insecurities to our kids, get ourselves into financial messes. Should I go on?

History is full of powerful leaders who created whole nations who participated in mass evil. So I don't agree when Christians say you can't do anything without God. A lot of people have made a name for themselves, and God got zero credit. There is a spiritual power that is real when we choose to come together as one. That spiritual power can be used for positive or negative.

My Cleveland Browns need to come together with positive power and finally win a championship! I'm an athlete, so I think in sports terms most of the time. Great teams and dynasties come together as one mind, and they accomplish amazing feats that others view as impossible.
What if we decided to take this truth and use it for God's purposes on earth? What if we viewed our marriage as a team designed to be one force that the world can't reckon with? What if we viewed our money as a tool to be used to accomplish things that bring glory to God rather than my name? What if …
Dream with me! Dream with your spouse! Dream with your kids! Dream with your business team! Dream with your church!

We have incredible power when we come together! The Scriptures teach that we have the power to bind and loose things. We limit and empower things every day in our own lives and the lives of others around us by what we say and do. The Scriptures also say if just two people agree on something and ask God for it, it will be done for them. Now I have heard this passage taught on many times and pastors are quick to bring in all kinds of qualifiers on this one to make sure our motives are pure. Hang with me on this one for a moment, let me push a little.

Let me first say; I am a believer in always understanding teachings from the context it was written. And the context for that truth of two people agreeing and asking God for something and getting it is how to heal broken relationships due to sinful or hurtful actions. What a powerful truth that we all have experienced in life: go directly to the person and talk it through together and own your part together and the relationship is stronger. Whether you realize it or not or even acknowledge it, that's God's spirit at work in your life! Thank him! There's a lot more where that came from that you can tap into my friend!

Knowing the context is important, but never limit God to what you are comfortable with, because in doing that we disempower others. I don't agree with everything everyone claims to be done for God or with God's blessing. I always look to God's written word as my guide for truth. There are teachings in scripture that we don't always like; there are things we want God to bless that are not his ways. And some truths are harder for some people to live out than others; we all have our own weaknesses and challenges to grow through. The purpose of this book is not to get into all of those types of things. But I do want to speak to an overall principle of truth that I believe has limited and weakened many believers. As a former pastor for over 20 years, one of the things that got under my skin quicker than anything else was when people who viewed themselves as mature Christians would act like they had the corner on faith.

Don't ever let anyone discourage you from trusting God to work in your life in miraculous ways. I've spent my entire life in the church, and people who grow up not experiencing God doing amazing things in their life tend to caution people out of a view of God that is protective rather than expansive. Some Christians are so afraid of being disappointed that they have a mindset of scarcity rather than abundance.

God is a creator, healer, provider, without limits! It's His character. So live every day believing that God will work in those ways in your life no matter what the circumstances look like or people say. That is not arrogant or selfish. Let God be the one to limit you if in His sovereignty, He decides, don't leave it up to other people. Live life on the proactive side of faith, not the reactive hesitant side. You get what you ask for! Seek, knock, look, and you will find!

I think the reason a lot of Christians tend to limit God and others is they are trying to protect people from sinning, from dishonoring God. That is the Holy Spirit's job; to convict us of sin and correct us and guide us. God doesn't parent us out of fear and negativity. He believes in us, trusts us, and allows us to make mistakes along the way to learn and grow. If we choose to not respond to His correction, He takes away our influence and power. God will not be mocked!

So believe the best for your life and in others. Inspire others to have faith that God is a healer, provider, and restorer! Your faith heals you! Believe God for great things and believe in yourself! Don't spend a minute debating about the what if's around your health because worry and fear only produce negative results.

Nobody knows how many days they have, so make the most of today no matter what happens and inspire others to do the same. I was told that I only had a 20% chance to live past five years back in 2011. Sorry, I don't focus on what I'm told I can't do!

Some people looked at me like I was a dreamer. Like I wasn't very serious or realistic. But I could sense their fear. I was not afraid. I know my God, and He loves me and has good plans for my life! Cancer just happened to be part of His good plan! And He's looking pretty good, isn't He! God loves a challenge because He has zero fear in Him. He is love! Love always conquers fear! So He's not shaken up when we doubt Him. He's been around the block many times over the centuries with all of His kids that think they are such smart realists who know how life works! Wink, wink!!!

Friends, I need to say something that we all need to hear! Sometimes God's good plan involves pain! All of Jesus' disciples ended up being martyrs for their faith, and they saw it as a blessing! Job was stricken with illness and lost his family in disasters, even though he was a Godly man!

Why can't we allow God to be good even when He uses difficult circumstances to accomplish His purposes? Remember, it's not about you and me! Sometimes the pain in our lives is because of our own doing, and sometimes it's not. It's not my place to try to tell you which it is. God's ultimate goal is not happiness; it's faithfulness. I want peace, love, and blessings just like you do, but not more than living a life that honors God. People read about natural disasters, plagues, sicknesses, wars in the Old Testament that God brought on the world as consequences for disobedience; leaders and nations who self-examined chose to repent and turn from ways that dishonored God. We are so quick to claim God's power when we like the results, saying God is love, like love doesn't ever cause pain! We all know that sometimes love hurts and even has to draw boundaries and use force to protect. Love is not just soft and good feelings! There are even New Testament examples of God causing people to die for many reasons, lying about giving more to the church than they claimed, being faithful witnesses to Christ in nations that killed people to try to scare them to reduce the ONE TRUE GOD. Can death, sickness, and disaster be a good thing?

I wouldn't wish cancer on anyone. Most of us wouldn't wish harm on others unless of course, someone deserves it for hurting us. We've all had some of those thoughts! But let's get one thing clear about

God. We are not His judge! So whether or not we understand why He is doing something in this world doesn't change the fact that He is GOOD and JUST! And yes, even when it's painful! I know my life will have more painful experiences, I have resolved that God is good, and I am okay no matter what I have to face because I'm not living for this life! When we live for eternity, we see a much bigger picture to this life! And we tend to accomplish incredible things by faith in this life!

I've learned to laugh now when people call me a dreamer or unrealistic. Because I have nothing to prove to others, I don't ignore present realities; I face them head-on and just choose to believe that they are subject to both the power of our Creator and our mind!

The invisible world is what sustains the visible world, so stop getting it backwards people! We all live by faith; the only question is, what are we putting our faith in? Learn how to move mountains; God wants you to. He told you to! It's more real than you think! There is a whole new world out there that is just waiting for you to walk into it! It's a lot more exciting, fulfilling, freeing and beautiful! Join me and let's move mountains together! Build your successful business, raise the next generation with confidence, be more in love with your wife of 30 years than honeymooners, be courageous sharing your faith with the world, this is what it means to be a believer! It's the only way people ever see the true God! You can't control the

ONE and ONLY TRUE GOD that I've introduced you to!

The other reason I believe I got cancer was because I had been stuck in a negative, victim mentality for a few years that affected my body and immune system in a destructive way that I believe positioned my body to reproduce unhealthy cells that developed into cancer.

Let me ask you a very frank question. How many people do you know that take ownership for getting a disease? People don't just go around saying I ate myself into Type 2 Diabetes, or I worried myself into chronic pain. I'm not saying we cause all of our sicknesses; I simply want to point out that we have full control of what we allow in our mind and body and these have a direct impact on our physical health.

There are many things that we are learning and will learn that go into mass processed food that is damaging to our bodies. It's why all-natural food stores are on the rise. We all know that pop is not good for you. We know we shouldn't eat as many sweets. But we don't talk enough about how our thinking affects our health. In fact, the majority of the time, we coddle each other with a victim mindset. We make excuses that we're so busy we have to eat fast food; we spend a lot of time complaining to coworkers each day about how bad our boss is, we even get easily offended on social media. The reason I am raising this point is because a victim mindset is one of the most limiting, disempowering, and destructive diseases we can be infected with! And it's a self-induced disease! Remember, my name is Fred, and I'm your friend!

James Allen, in his book *As a Man Thinketh*, talks about how strong; pure, positive thoughts build up the body and how sickly thoughts will express itself through a sickly body. [5] The Scriptures talk about the effects of our mindset on our body also. Proverbs 17:22 "*A cheerful heart is good medicine, but a crushed spirit dries up the bones.*" One of the things I have learned through my cancer and from other challenges in my life is that a victim mindset always sets us up for failure, whether it's relationally, physically, or professionally.

Before my cancer, I was living out my calling of reaching the northeast side of Indianapolis for Christ. We were growing a church that was very intentional at meeting people where they were at in life and introducing them to a God who loved them and had great plans for their life! We had baptized hundreds of people, grown to over 600 people at Easter and were about ten years into growing this movement, and we hit some challenging situations.

The market crash of 2008 hit us financially, and we had to let go of some staff, which was very difficult. Six months after that, the church elders and I had to let go of our associate pastor for inappropriate behavior. He was one of my best friends and my trust was broken. It deeply hurt me and the church community.

In order to take some time to heal personally and help the church heal, I brought on a dear friend Rolland Daniels, who had been a mentor of mine for years! He was a tremendous gift to our church! I was struggling with the church plateauing, and I wasn't enjoying the role of pastoring vs. planting a church. I've always been drawn to evangelism; I'm entrepreneurial by nature. I love starting things and growing organizations that impact people's lives. The daily pastoral role was not energizing, but I loved the people. I found myself stuck. I've since realized that my insecurities caused me to think I needed people too much.

I think of the story of Moses, who was insecure about his speaking abilities and kept telling God I can't do this, he told God five times! Finally, God got mad and decided to use his brother Aaron as the spokesperson. And how did that work out for him? Not so good!

Aaron misled the people multiple times, once to worship a bull they created from their gold jewelry while God was giving The Ten Commandments! Another time Aaron and his sister questioned Moses' leadership, causing the Israelites to doubt him, God settled that one definitively who He had chosen as the leader!

As I study Moses' life, his insecurities caused him a lot of pain and even his ultimate calling! He was supposed to lead God's people into the Promised Land, but they refused to follow his leadership and trust God and multiple times God told Moses He was going to destroy them all and start over with their kids, Moses stopped God every time. Every sermon I've ever heard preached on this was from a place of care for his people like this was a good thing: that a human knew better than God or that a human was more loving than God.

But the result of his own decisions caused Moses to get mad at his people, so he didn't do what God told him to do and blamed them for him not getting into the Promised Land. Have you ever found yourself blaming other people for your lack of faith in God? I find it fascinating that Moses spent all of his time debating with God instead of trusting Him. He was the one who argued with God instead of trusting Him. God gave him what he wanted, and in the end, Moses didn't like the results.

Why did Moses do this? I think he had a bigger need to be accepted by his people than by God. I feel a little sacrilegious even making that statement because Moses is in the Hall of Fame chapter of men and women who lived by faith in the book of Hebrews! God did some amazing things through him! Yet as I read his story of being adopted by the Pharaoh and raised in royalty then as a grown man trying to defend his people by killing an Egyptian who was beating an Israelite slave and being told by his own people you're not one of us, are you going to kill us too? He was never accepted by his own people; they constantly rejected him and God. All of this and Moses still wanted that approval; he thought he needed that security. And it cost him!

I identify with Moses! God used my cancer to get me to step away from Northeast and my insecurities of thinking I was not a strong communicator and that I needed someone to come alongside me in order to fulfill my call. I learned that I was limiting myself! God actually freed me and gave me a new opportunity to start over and lead from a place of confidence in myself as a communicator and leader and not to have to make it about me being accepted! I kind of think of it as Northeast 2.0 on steroids!

I know who I am and who I'm not. And I'm good with that! I'm a connector, not a manager. My vision is now way bigger than it was before. What God wants me to do has nothing to do with how great I am, but yet at the same time, I've never felt more confident in who I am and know that people will come and go, but I have made the decision not to let my faith be limited by a need for others. That allows me to love people and speak truth to them. God will take care of the rest! He's got me!

Before this change in thinking, most of my thoughts were from a negative, victim mindset. When we think this way, it shuts off our creative capacity and ability to inspire others to join us. We also tend to close ourselves off from the needed support of people who are already where we want to go. I had some good mentors in my life, but I didn't know how to use them well. I wasn't a very good listener. I would just vent.

I've learned to use mentors as a sounding board now, asking them what they think I can learn from where I'm currently at, rather than just complaining.

I'm very thankful for where I am now in life and actually love the things I get to do and feel like my call is bigger than ever, it's just not in the church now, it's out in the business world, which I love since I'm an evangelist at heart and an entrepreneur. But that season of life for a few years I was stuck, and it affected my body. I wasn't my usual fun-loving, positive, confident, faith-oriented visionary leader. My negative, victim mentality took its toll on my body. I read a lot about how our mind and body works and the science behind our beliefs. One of the common threads I find in all the books I read is that science shows that our bodies respond to our positive and negative emotions and actually reproduces what we believe.

In his book, The Biology of Belief, Dr. Bruce Lipton shares how his study and many other biologists are finding that as our cells die and reproduce that they are dramatically impacted by our thinking. [6]

Science used to claim that our DNA was set, now we are finding that our thoughts positively or negatively affect the development of new cell growth! We are not stuck having to blame our genetics in life! We have complete control over our mindset, and that gives us the power to create a positive, healthy body! It's called epigenetics, which means above our genes!

Athletes know, you never let your body tell you that you are tired or that you can't do something. Champions, people who grow and succeed, tell their body to push through pain and limits. If we want to get stronger physically, we have to lift weights we've never done before and work harder than before; it's how growth happens. All of this starts with a mindset first. We cannot be weak-minded, or we will complain and quit.

I would encourage you to speak life and health and strength to yourself every day. Your body will respond to what you believe. If you think you're immune system is bad it will be. If you worry about getting sick, you will create symptoms that you worry about. Your body produces what your mind fixates on. If you think healthy thoughts, you will want to eat better and exercise because your body will produce what you choose to dwell on.

To find out if you have a positive or negative mindset with health, do a little personal assessment. Record how many times in a day that you think positive or negative things or say positive or negative things about your health. Just tally them each day for two weeks. At the same time, record how many times you feel sick or bad during those two weeks. See if there is a correlation. What do you think when you have a pain or an ailment? Do you find yourself naturally thinking something is wrong and spend time wondering what it could be or even researching? If so your body is getting negative messages from you that something is wrong so it will produce more of those symptoms.

On the other hand, when you have aches and pains, if you think positively and continue to exercise and do the things that build strength your body will respond and in turn send endorphins that produce health and energy. I'm not saying deny symptoms or real sickness; I'm just saying we make ourselves sick or a lot sicker when we dwell on it. Your body needs you to be it's first and best defense, so be positive and do the things that build strength mentally and physically every day.

I spend time every day reading in God's word and praying, but just as important for me is exercise. When I work out, it is my way of also growing spiritually because I work through frustrations and push myself, and it helps me to let go of stress and grow in confidence. I'm 50, and my goal is to be working out just as much when I am in my 70's because it keeps me mentally stronger and energized! I often go up to older people who are working out in gyms and tell them that they are my hero's because my goal is to be working out when I'm their age, they usually get a big smile and say I'm just trying to stay active!

Decide right now that you are going to take full responsibility for your health! That you are not going to have a victim mentality and blame or make excuses for how you eat or lack of exercise or mental laziness. Believe that you have the power to influence your health in a positive, life-giving direction and do everything that you can to motivate yourself! Most people wait until something bad happens to change, and their bodies are not ready for it. If you do end up facing health issues, you will be better for it if you have built strong disciplines into your life!

Quit eating crap! Quit drinking pop and beer! Quit smoking! Quit using food as comfort! Quit using pornography as a release to feel good! Quit telling your family and friends all of your excuses for why you are not healthy! Quit telling yourself the lie that some people just have better genetics and metabolism; it's a cop-out! Quit making your doctor and the pharmacist so wealthy by thinking and doing things that make you indebted to sickness. Quit everything that has control over you! And quit denying that you have a problem! Remember, my name is Fred, and I'm your friend!

What if we could spend as much time and money talking about and doing positive things that build health rather than complaining and whining about all of our health problems and how much money we have to spend?

Just think about how much more time you could spend helping other people and making a positive impact with your time and money rather than being focused on yourself. Ouch! I know that one stings, but it's the truth!

You're wasting your time, other people's time and God's time! I know that because God's advice in scripture over and over again is, Be strong and courageous, get to work doing what I made you to do! Health starts in your mind. Learn to be the master of your mind! It makes life much more fun and energizing and rewarding! Blessings!

SECTION TWO

THE
FIGHT
BEGINS

ROUND 1: SURGERY ... LET'S DO THIS!

My wife and I were in the prep room, waiting for the doctor to call me back to surgery. We had already prayed together, and I was ready to go under the knife for the first time in my life. The nurse walked in and said, "Your pastor is here to see you." I looked at Dyan with a confused look and then said to the nurse, "I'm the pastor of my church."

When you are a pastor, you shoulder the responsibility of caring for others. People look to you in times of need. It's a privilege to be seen as a spiritual leader in other people's eyes, but it also carries a weight to it, and if you don't seek out older wiser mentors to build into you it's easy to burn out in ministry. I had spent the past few weeks encouraging our church members that things were going to be okay, so I was in the mindset of caring for others.

Then in walked Rolland Daniels, my dear friend who had been on our staff and been a mentor and friend for years! Instantly I felt a sense of God's loving care on my life. I was able to take off my pastor hat and have a spiritual leader that I looked up to speak into our lives and pray and minister to us with his presence!

One of the things pastors understand is the power of presence! Families feel safer when a pastor walks in the room and spends time connecting with them. You don't even have to say much. Just being there says you matter!

If there is one thing I wish more people would have confidence in, it's that their presence has the power to show God's love to others! Most people say things like, I'm not a pastor, or I don't know what to say. NO, NO, NO, please hear me on this one, any act of love you do for God has the power to change a life! Whether it's just taking the time to visit someone, cook a meal, say an encouraging word, send a card, every small act can have a great impact!

God uses people to show his love and truth! You are God's representative! Pastors are people just like you that have an important role to play, but your role is just as important, in fact, I have learned over the years that your role is a role that a pastor cannot play! There are people that only you can reach! There are people that you have influence over. There are people that you are uniquely gifted and positioned to speak into! NEVER underestimate your role and power you can bring to change a person's life for good! Use your presence to minister to people!

I don't remember much after leaving Dyan. I vaguely remember them telling me to count to 10 and then before I knew it I was awake in the recovery room seeing my beautiful bride's smile! The early report was positive; the surgeon thought he had gotten all of the cancer cells around my knee. He told us they made a small incision in my right groin and took out two lymph nodes that they would send to be tested and would call us in a week to let us know that pathology report.

I was given strict instructions not to bend my knee the first few weeks since they had cut a football-shaped area out of the inside of my knee and then stretched the skin together. I had a 6-inch incision that was stitched up. I do remember the area being very tight for a long time, and looking like a whole chunk of my leg was missing. I was also introduced to compression hose for the first time! I called them pantyhose because that's what they looked like to me!

I had to wear them all the time, so I didn't get swelling in my leg. It took some getting used to the constriction feeling. I was supposed to keep my leg up as much as possible during the recovery period, which was about a month so I was in a wheelchair a lot, then used crutches for short walks around the house.

I remember coaching my son's championship game in a wheelchair, which we won! Luke was in 3rd grade and was our power running back. The kids played both ways since we only had 13 on a team, so he also played linebacker on defense, and he loved to hit people. I wasn't going to miss those games for anything! I love football, and it's very special getting to watch my son play a sport that he also loves.

My good friend Mike Taylor was my assistant coach, and his son, Nick, was our quarterback. Nick brought the speed around the end and had a good arm throwing the ball and then my son, Luke got tough yards up the middle. The triple threat of power, speed, and passing made it very difficult for teams to stop us and ended up winning us 3 out of 4 championships against one of my other close friends Chris Cochran, who we faced every year!

Growing up, my dad never missed one sporting event I played in: football, basketball, wrestling, baseball, and track. When I played college football at Anderson University, my parents never missed one game in 4 years driving over 5hrs one way every week, sometimes up to 14hrs! Then he would drive back the same day and get home late and preach the next morning. My parents instilled in me a strong sense of involvement with your family. There was no question how much they cared and loved me!

As I became an adult, I made a decision that I was going to be present in my kids' lives. When Dyan and I sensed God calling us to plant a new church in Fishers, Indiana, I knew how hard it was to build something from the ground up. I made the promise that I would not work more than 50 hours a week and would be home most evenings and not miss my kids' activities.

I believed that God would bless me more for being a present husband and father than putting my career and success ahead of family and asking God to make up the difference with my loved ones. God will never honor that type of deal; you can't replace a spouse or a parent! You can replace a boss, manager, a salesman, a secretary and even a pastor.

I read a very short book by Andy Stanley before I planted the church called *Choosing to Cheat*. His premise in the book is we all cheat somewhere with our time; never cheat family! Based on his advice and my parents' example, I made a commitment to never cheat my family. I've never regretted that decision! I've experienced a lot of success in my work and am more in love with my wife of 27 years than ever, and we are close with all of our kids! We have so many fond memories we laugh about and pictures we text back and forth to each other from our life growing up as a family!

When I went back to see the doctor a week later to see how the incision was healing on my knee, we discovered it was having a little trouble coming together and scabbing over. I remember the doctor sternly getting on me telling me I'm not following the instructions of not bending my knee. I told him "No, I've followed all the instructions!:" He shot back, "No, you are not!" I looked at my wife like I wanted to deck him, and she assured the doctor that I had been doing everything he had told me to do. Then he said, "Well, you're not doing it good enough!" He was concerned that things wouldn't heal properly and could get infected.

Within the next few weeks, the skin started healing up; it was just so stretched that it took a while for it to come together. I remember having to massage it later to loosen up the tightness, which took a long time! At that same appointment, the doctor shared the results of the pathology report from my lymph nodes they had tested. We were not ready to hear what came next!

ROUND 2: IT'S SPREADING

"One of your lymph nodes tested positive. Your cancer has spread!"

If there is any news scarier than, "You have cancer, " it's, "Your cancer has spread!" After hearing those words, the doctor went on to explain how Stage 4 was your internal organs, which cannot be surgically removed. When malignant melanoma is at this stage, there is no real treatment. This form of cancer is known in the medical community as a serious killer! It's very important to catch it early. You cannot do laser treatment; chemo doesn't work on it. There are only some experimental drugs you can try that don't have much clinical proof of success (I'll talk more about this in the next chapter).

So my diagnosis was Stage 3, just before your internal organs. Things got much more serious very quickly. The prognosis did not look good! Hearing the news that your cancer had spread was deflating! The doctor went on to explain that your lymph nodes are part of your circulatory system. They circulate fluids throughout your body and prevent your limbs from swelling. They also help with part of your immune system sending needed soldiers to fight off infections throughout your body. So when the glands in your neck or groin or armpits are swollen, that is a sign that your body is fighting off something.

When you hear news like, your cancer has spread, your mind kind of goes numb and you just say things like "uh-huh," "okay," as the doctor explains more details. Your mind starts racing with all kinds of questions and concerns. After the doctor finished sharing, he said that I needed to have a second surgery to remove all of the lymph nodes in my right groin, it's called a lymphadenectomy. He told me that we needed to let my leg heal up before doing the next surgery, so we set a follow-up surgery date for three weeks later.

I remember walking out of that appointment and getting into the elevator with Dyan, and we looked at each other and grabbed hands, and both said, "We will get through this! God is with us, and we can do this!"

We both had a very strong sense of being up for the challenge. Even though the news was a low blow, we quickly decided to get on the side of focusing on what we could do and trusting that the rest was in God's hands.

Let me pause for just a minute and speak to those moments in life when you didn't see that punch coming! You know those moments when you get the breath knocked out of you; when the wind is taken out of your sails. You know what I'm talking about! When someone tells you something or does something that you never imagined you would hear or have to deal with. What you do in those moments, the decisions you make in your heart right then and there determines everything!

You see, our beliefs about life get formed in one of two ways — sudden emotional impacts, like traumatic events, or space repetition of time - habitual exposure to the same thing over and over. Most of our core beliefs, which most of us are not aware of, are formed out of fear. The majority of people live their lives driven by fear, and they don't realize it and deny that that could be true! Remember, my name is Fred, and I am your friend!

Why do we worry about things? Fear of losing something, security. Why do we let people pressure us and then resent them? Fear of being rejected. Why do we lash out at people that we love the most? Fear of being taken advantage of. Why do we close off to people? Fear of criticism. It's really okay to admit that much of life is driven by fear because you're not alone! And the only way to change it is first to become aware and admit it! It's actually very freeing! It also builds tremendous strength.

You see, we live in fear when we have a scarcity mindset. There's not enough; I'm not good enough, nobody cares about me, I have to do it all, or it won't get done, where was God when I needed him?

A scarcity mindset is motivated by fear. So, we give up; we don't even try, we isolate ourselves, we don't trust people, we close ourselves off to God and others. This mindset steals our ambition for life; we quit, we become passive, negative, critical, easily discouraged, easily angered, passive-aggressive, and weak-minded.

But if we are honest with ourselves and can identify limiting, negative beliefs that hold us back in fear, we can then replace those lies with the truth. The truth is an abundance mindset, and it is motivated by love! Love drives out fear! Love rejoices in the truth! Love always protects! Love always trusts! Love inspires hope! Love develops persistent strength! Love always wins!

Love doesn't fear lack! Love doesn't grow insecurity! Love isn't harsh! Love doesn't retaliate! Love doesn't control! Love doesn't avoid! Love doesn't focus on what's wrong! Love doesn't doubt! Love empowers us to dream, succeed, step up, and step out. Love believes, adds value, sees the positive, and affirms. Love is confident, patient, caring, kind, and mentally strong!

So, when life throws you a curveball you didn't expect, what mindset do you draw from? Scarcity or Abundance? Fear or Love? Doubt or Faith? There is no ½ way; you are one or the other! This is a choice we get to make! NEVER blame life for your choices! You choose what you already believe about life, so circumstances simply give you a chance to show what you really believe. Be a fighter! Be someone who unites people! Be a force for good! Be a believer!

We chose to believe God had us, so we put on our gloves for round two! My parents drove out to this surgery; it was an inpatient overnight stay. I was on dozens of church prayer chains, and I could sense the support and love of others praying. Deep down, I had confidence that the doctor would remove the rest, and I would get on with how God wanted to use my life to help others. I was 41 years old and had never had a surgery, and now I was going in for my second in one month's time. After leaving Dyan, the next thing I remembered was waking up with an itching and burning sensation in my groin and the inside of my thigh.

Before I got to go home, the nurse changed my bandages and gave me instructions on cleaning the incision. I remember being startled at seeing dozens of staples along the 12 inch incision in my groin. I thought they would use stitches. The staples were uncomfortable at times, pinching a little. I also had a drain tube that came out of my leg halfway down my thigh, which was weird and awkward to deal with.

When I went home, our friends had given us a walker for me to use in the house, which turned out to be much easier to get around with than crutches. One of my favorite pictures was of me standing with my walker and compression hose striking a bicep flex in our living room! That post got a lot of likes on Facebook! I also had a blog where I posted daily thoughts since I was not able to get around for a month. This was a great way to connect with others and channel my time constructively while my body was healing.

My incision healed very well this time! When I went to get the staples out, the doctor said, "This will pinch a little." It was not fun; I believe I had 24 staples in total! I did have a few questions for the doctor, especially about the numbness in my inner thigh. I couldn't feel anything but would have these sensations of itching and scratching did nothing for it. I also had this feeling of tingling when I would touch the area or if the area was bumped. The doctor said I would have some nerve damage due to all the cutting that was done. To this day, I still have very little feeling in my inner thigh.

I wore compression hose for the better part of a year and had to go to massage therapy where they taught me how to help the fluid move out of my leg. At the end of the day water pools where my sock stops and the kids used to think it was fun to push in on my leg and see the indent of their finger! My leg and feet get swollen easily due to not having any lymph nodes on that side of my groin. My chubby foot is my little reminder of God's grace in my life!

I have been able to exercise and still do sports, and my circulation does pretty well! After a month of healing up from the second surgery, it was time to get started on preventative treatments. Up until this point, things went very well, and the biggest challenge was being bored recovering at home! But everything in my life was about to take a turn that I was not ready for and set a lot of other things in motion that rocked my world!

ROUND 3: A NEW TREATMENT

Your life becomes one medical procedure or visit after another when you have cancer. One day you're doing what you want then all of a sudden doctors and nurses schedule your calendar. I briefly mentioned there is no radiation or chemo that works on malignant melanoma skin cancer. The only treatment they had tested was a drug called *Interferon*. It's a very powerful drug! The only studies they found were patients who took the drug for six months to a year had a 20% less chance of cancer returning within five years. Not really promising, but it was the only preventative medication.

The drug was usually administered three times a week through infusion, and it would leave your system within 24 hours. They had just come out with a new form of the drug where you took a shot once a week, and it stayed in your bloodstream all week. My insurance would not allow me to take the old drug, so I ended up being the first patient in Indiana ever to take the drug. My oncologist shared with my wife and I all of the potential side effects of the drug: nausea, loss of appetite, weight loss, low sex drive, anxiety, depression, and in severe cases potentially insomnia and suicidal thoughts.

They explained that the drug is killing your cells, and it caused your body to release the chemicals of fear and doom. We met with a drug specialist who recommended that I take a low dose of antidepressant just to be precautionary. We talked about it, I didn't like some of the potential side effects (I like sex), and I was a very positive, optimistic and energetic person, so I decided that we would wait and see how I felt.

The first month they had me come in to get the shot, then after that, I started giving myself the shot at home and would see the doctor to check my levels every other week. I remember the first time I got the shot. Dyan went with me, and I remember it taking a long time because we were heading to my older son, Seth's, basketball game afterward. Things went well, and I thought this isn't so bad! During the first half of the game, I started to get a little cold and was shivering, then at halftime, I was sweating, and Dyan looked at me and said, "We have got to get you home! You are green!" My body was fighting the new drug; when I looked in the mirror, I thought wow is this Gamma? I looked like the hulk, not his size, but green! After breaking the sweat that evening and returning to my normal color, I felt fine.

The first month went pretty smoothly. I went in once a week for a shot and to get my levels tested. In fact, I was feeling so good that I even flew down to North Carolina in December to do the wedding for my cousin Kimberly who was marrying RJ. I had been doing online marriage counseling with them for the past few months. It was a very special time celebrating with them and the rest of our extended family, and the car rental place upgraded me to a convertible mustang! It was a fun weekend!

After the first month, I started giving myself a shot at home every Sunday night. I remember the first time I went to get the prescription; it came in small vials. Each vial was enough for one shot. When we got our first medical bill, we were floored when we saw that each vial cost $10,000! Fortunately, we had good insurance through Dyan's work. In fact, that was another major God moment. The week we found out about my cancer was the week Dyan's new insurance took effect! Before that, we had private insurance since I was a self-employed pastor. There is no such thing as coincidence when it comes to the timing of things that work out! There is a God who is watching out for us and works details out that we could never have seen ahead of time!

ROUND 4: SIDE EFFECTS

The next few months went really well! I was still working out three times a week and pastoring the church. What I did not realize was that the drug had a compounding effect over time. I didn't realize how much it was affecting me at first. I had lost some of my appetite, so I started drinking protein drinks as a supplement. It was 2-3 months before I started experiencing more of the side effects. Then things started to compound over time.

I started to find myself feeling unsure of myself and hesitant with decisions, which was not me! I started to lose weight, I was already skinny at 6ft 175lbs, but ended up losing over 25lbs in three months.

Then the mental effects started. I would feel anxious and nervous, during this time, I was talking with another local church planter Dave Sumrall, who was reaching hundreds of people for Christ. We would dream together about reaching our city for Christ, and I worked out with his team. I began to think that maybe we should join together. After many discussions with our Elders and then a church meeting we decided to move forward, and I remember the day after deciding to dissolve *Northeast* and join *iTown* I had a panic attack! I had never had a panic attack before.

My sister in law Suzi had dealt with panic attacks when she went through her cancer the first time. My wife experienced panic attacks while staying with her dad in the ER and then the ICU before he passed away. Dyan had post-traumatic stress flashbacks and anxiety attacks for a while. I had never experienced anything like that before. Being an athlete and an optimist, I always thought, just think about the positive side and move on! For the first time in my life that didn't work for me!

I remember getting this tingling feeling up the back of my neck, and I would be overcome with fear and doom. That is exactly what the drug counselor had said *Interferon* produces in your body. I remember having ruminating thoughts of negativity and felt trapped. I started experiencing depression. That was scary! I remember feeling like I couldn't make myself pull out of it. My chemicals were off in my brain, and I wasn't able to manage basic life circumstances. Because I had ruminating thoughts, I couldn't sleep. I actually went two solid weeks without sleeping. I felt like I was going crazy! Insomnia is where your brain doesn't stop; I would try to make myself think I was tired. Eventually, this all led to becoming suicidal. I was scared to be with anyone other than Dyan, which put a tremendous amount of pressure on her!

I would tell Dyan I'm afraid to be by myself. I didn't have a plan, but I didn't trust myself because I wasn't thinking right. I was so tired and scared that I didn't know what I would do. Everything finally came to a head when we were over in Dayton, Ohio visiting her mom for Memorial Day weekend. We were taking family pictures with all of the extended family in the backyard and in between pictures I would go back inside and tell Dyan I need to go to the hospital. As soon as we finished the pictures, she took me to the emergency room, and they put me on an IV with morphine. I remember a few things that stood out about that night.

First, they put people to watch guard in my room. I had three different people that rotated shifts. The first person I had was a young lady in her 20's; her name was Chelsea. I told her I had a daughter named Chelsea, and it made me feel like God was watching out for me! Then I had this big African American guy who looked like a bouncer. He was really funny and told me he wouldn't let anything happen to me. He talked to me about God and guardian angels. I felt very safe with him as my guardian angel. Then the last person I had was an older lady; she had a calming presence about her like my grandma was praying for me!

The other thing I remember about that night was the doctor whispering to Dyan around 1:30 in the morning that he wasn't sure what more he could do because he had already given me three rounds of morphine and I still wasn't asleep yet. The drug *Interferon* had really messed with my mind! Finally, I did get a little bit of sleep.

Then when we went back home, I checked into an outpatient stress center and decided that I was done with *Interferon*. The side effects were not worth continuing. Our original plan was to take the drug for one year. We stopped at six months, and I was told it would take one month to get it fully out of my system. I spent the next year and a half recovering from mental depression.

ROUND 5: DEPRESSION & MENTAL ILLNESS

Mental Illnesses still have a stigma about them because people don't understand them. We tend to be afraid of what we don't understand. Remember, most of society doesn't know their real purpose in life and worries about what other people think about them. It takes self-confidence to admit weaknesses and address issues that society deems taboo. Some people also have the warped belief that if you talk about the realities of mental illness, it will in some way, make things worse. There are also a lot of religious views that can make depression and mental illness even harder and lonelier to deal with. Many well-meaning people say things like; you don't need medicine; you just need more faith. So let's pause and take a moment to address meds and faith and public perception. Let's identify some negative lies that limit us and reframe things in a way that speak truth and life into a world that desperately needs some help!

Some lies we believe:

- You aren't normal if you struggle with depression.
- You should be able to just deal with it.
- Meds are a crutch; faith is all you need.
- Keep quiet about it, so you don't embarrass yourself and the family.
- If people find out you could lose your job.
- Men are weak if they struggle with depression.

The list could go on and on. There are multiple reasons people can experience depression and mental illness: hereditary genetics, traumatic life experiences, dishonesty, unhealthy boundaries with others, drug addictions, to name a few. Some of the causes are not our fault; other causes can be our own doing.

Either way, you can find help and healing! I will share the three most important steps you can take no matter what the reason is.

First, whether you feel it or not, tell yourself positive self-talk. Speak out loud life-giving statements about your worth and mental strength and stability. And say them in the present tense like you have it! Don't make I wish or want statements, your subconscious mind that controls your beliefs runs on autopilot. So you have to reprogram your core beliefs with truth. Truth is not a future reality; it is a present spiritual power that can override faulty programing. I believe that truth lies in the person of Jesus Christ. The scriptures say that the truth will set you free and that where the Spirit of the Lord is there is freedom. Depression and Mental Illness trap us into unhealthy, negative images of ourselves that steals truth and hope.

One way to grow toward mastering your mind is to read the Bible's promises of God. There are hundreds of them, and He repeats many of them like: I love you, I will never leave you or forsake you, and you are more than conquerors in Christ.

Listen to speakers and people who build you up. I know that when you are in the middle of depression, you feel helpless; I lived in that ocean for over a year. But I still quoted scriptures and intentionally listened to people who spoke life into me. I can remember driving to work for over a year praying and quoting scriptures like; I can do all things through Christ who gives me strength. I did not feel it or even believe it, but I kept saying it out loud to myself. It eventually clicked. One of my favorite scriptures is Isaiah 55:11 *"Every time my word goes out from my mouth it will not return to me empty, but it will accomplish what I desire and achieve the purpose for which I sent it."* There is power in God's spoken word when we speak it; it changes us!

In later chapters called *Build Disciplines* and *Mental Mastery*, I will talk about how to master your mind and share some scriptures that God designed to help us build up and protect our mind from the negative messages we often feel about ourselves.

A second step we can take to overcome depression and mental illness is reaching out to trusted friends for support and getting professional help! We need one another, and I'm not talking about just in our weak moments, we were designed by God to be in relationship with other people. God said from the very beginning in Genesis, the first book of the Bible that it's not good for man to be alone. Depression and mental illness win when we isolate ourselves. Depression is an internal battle. When we wrestle with thoughts alone inside our head, we get stuck and feel shame, like we are not worth anything. This is a lie. We need other people in our life to counter the messages we feel and believe about ourselves. My wife was unbelievably strong for me when I was battling depression. She loved me, pushed me, and connected me with people who could help!

There are wonderful stress centers all around full of trained, caring people who know how to walk through mental illnesses with you! And let me say it straight up, as a third step, mental illness requires medical help! God uses medicine to aid in the healing process! It is not our savior, but God has allowed us to find answers to scientific realities that are going on in our brain. We know that there are chemicals in our brain, and sometimes those levels are not balanced and produce a depressed state of mind. When your levels are off, we can't manage life and stress properly. It would be equivalent to someone who did not have arms trying to shoot a basketball. They do not have the tools needed to accomplish the task. The needed chemical is missing, so, therefore, we cannot counter our feelings of despondency with rational optimism.

We accept this reality when we can see it physically. But we have a very hard time with mental illness because we can't see the missing arm! But it's missing! In fact, sometimes all that people need to help them overcome their struggle is knowing that others understand their reality and don't look down on them because of it. Antidepressants function to correct the chemical imbalance and allow people to play on a level playing field. This doesn't solve the problem, but it does allow us to be able to choose to focus on the positive. We still have to do the mental work of thinking healthy.

Many family members have a history of depression, but it wasn't treated, and there was way more suffering than there needed to be. When the drug *interferon* messed with my chemical balance in my brain, I was not able to just change my thinking. I had to try a few different antidepressants, which was a slow and frustrating process since it takes a few weeks to take effect, and the first one I tried made my struggle worse. I quickly learned about how some antidepressants actually lower you and others lift you. We were finally able to get the right mix, and then I also had to take a medication for my ruminating thoughts. After months of monitoring my medication, I started to get some relief, I am very thankful for my psychiatrist; I ended up taking the medication for over two years and slowly tapered off after that during the third year.

I remember being very hesitant and fearful of going off the last medication, worrying about going back to how I felt before. It took time to build up my confidence to where I felt like myself again. My depression was driven by my treatment and situational circumstances. People who have low genetic levels often need to stay on low maintenance levels for consistency, and there is nothing weak or unspiritual about that! Can God heal depression and help you not need medication? Yes he can! But there is nothing wrong with using the discoveries we have made in science to help if needed!

Depression and mental illness are real, and if not taken seriously can lead to suicidal thoughts. We can find help and healing. I would bet at least one person in your family struggles with some form of mental illness, and you may not even know. You may have felt things for a long time and not known what to do. Every extended family is touched by this, and it's not bad to talk about it! Quit trying to cover up things worrying about what others will think and trying to act like your family is perfect! Get on the solution side of helping others find hope and victory!

ROUND 6: RECOVERY ... THE JOURNEY BACK

Getting back to myself was a long journey! Cancer and surgeries were not the hard part for me. It was recovering from what the drugs did to my mind and body! Along with the career change, I was faced with a huge financial pay cut and questions about who I was and how to start over at 42 years old!

So after my weekend in the hospital recovering from insomnia and severe depression that left me suicidal, I began an outpatient program at a stress center. I remember being embarrassed that I had to be a part of a recovery program for mental illness. I did not enjoy the group sessions because I just felt like everyone shared how they were the victim and it was actually more depressing for me to sit and listen to the same story repeated over and over. It motivated me to focus on more positive thoughts!

It took a few months to get my medications right to where I could function being with other people. Dyan and I took a trip to Colorado, and it was very refreshing to get away and enjoy nature. I slowly started feeling more positive feelings, but still was not able to handle anything challenging. When I came back from our trip, I started transitioning to a new role with the church we merged with and struggled to find my confidence. The building we were in was being transformed into a new look and there were many memories that I felt I was losing. I just wasn't ready to lead others yet, so I talked with Pastor Dave and decided it was best that I step down from my position so I could recover.

It was a very difficult transition that created a perfect storm of adding to what I was already struggling with mentally from the *Interferon*. I felt like I had failed God in my calling and failed the people we had reached at our church. Plus I was struggling with depression, and now had to find some kind of work that would take care of my family. Not to mention starting over on the pay scale. All of this left me feeling like a failure in most areas of my life: career, provider for my family, relationally with people. I don't blame anyone for what happened, I wouldn't wish any of the things I went through on anyone, but I can honestly say I am thankful for what I went through because I am more clear on who I am and my calling is bigger than ever! It took a few years to get there, though.

I went through all the stages of grief: denial, anger, bargaining, depression, and finally, acceptance. I can remember bargaining with God about getting back into pastoring and being angry that I had to try jobs that didn't seem to have purpose for me. I didn't know who I was if I wasn't a pastor, that's all I had ever done since I was 20 years old. I remember meeting monthly for over a year with my pastor and friend Andy Stephenson to process through things. I had another friend who had retired early and gotten into insurance sales. He was doing well and asked me if I would want to try it. I didn't want to do it, but our family needed me to provide what I could. I hated it. I traveled all around the state of Indiana, trying to convince senior citizens to buy life insurance policies and set up wills. There was a lot of pressure and a lot of details. I'm not a detail guy. And I only like selling things I deeply believe in. I did alright. It took a while for some income to roll in, but it was 100% commission, and I just wasn't ready for that while struggling with depression and not feeling confident in who I was.

I had a very dear friend, Jon Isaacs, who was also in between jobs during this time. He would call me to check-in. One day he came over to the house and spent the day hanging with me talking, playing cards, and just encouraging me! It was very special because Jon was one of the first guys I had the privilege of leading to Christ and baptizing when we planted *Northeast*! Jon and his wife Laura are like family to us! They have spent the past 25 years as our vacation and boating buddies! We have shared a lot of life together, and I am so grateful for their friendship over the years and the support they gave during a very difficult season! We call them lifers!

I gave insurance sales six months then transitioned into renewing my teaching license that I had never used from undergrad per my wife's suggestion. I have found after 27 years of marriage that God often speaks through a good wife! I took a few months and completed two online courses and then applied for over 20 elementary jobs in the area. I was still very insecure and lacking confidence but was able to push myself to do what I had to, complaining and afraid each step of the way.

People who know me have a hard time believing that because I am always the one who encourages everyone and loves to take risks. But depression masks the real personality of a person. It traps you! Makes you feel like you will never be able to smile or have hope again! It's a very lonely and scary feeling!

I can remember walking into services at Pendleton Christian Church with little hope and feeling like I was in a safe place! The friendships and Pastor Jay Harvey were a huge support during that difficult year! I remember having multiple conversations with Jay trying to make sense of all I was trying to recover from. And Devin Dummel was a gift to our family as our kid's youth pastor! Our kids loved Northeast and their youth pastors Candace and Andy Stephenson, so it was a very hard change for them to attend a new church and youth group. Fortunately, our kids went to Pendleton Heights High School and knew a lot of kids already from PCC. We remember meeting Devin in the lobby our first week to visit the church, and it was his first week on the job. We made a connection that has grown to where our daughter asked him to perform her wedding six years later! I love how God places people in your life to speak hope and life to you!

I was very fortunate to receive multiple phone calls for interviews. I believe there are three reasons. First, God was working things out ahead of me. You may not believe in God, but after I share some of the things that happened you will understand why I am such a firm believer that God is always working a plan for our lives for good! The second reason I believe I received so many opportunities is because I was a man, and there are very few men in elementary education. It's desperately needed for kids to have positive male role models at a young age. The third reason was I have spent my life investing in other people, and some very good people returned the favor recommending me to some principals. Tom Warmke, who had been one of my Elders at my church, and a former Superintendent, made some phone calls for me and one of them was the call God used to cause that Principal to give me a shot.

All four of my interviews came in early June and within the same week! The first one was on Monday at the school my kids went through. I did not get a callback. The second one was on Tuesday, almost an hour away, where my wife was a school counselor. The principal, Bev, knew me because I had visited Dyan a few times a year for special occasions. The school was in a small town with a depressed economy and lots of challenges! The majority of students did not have both parents, and many of them were in jail or on drugs. Bev is an incredible leader, and she tirelessly did everything she could to have the best school you could offer. I loved her energy and positivity! The meeting was with a few other teachers. It went really well, so well in fact, that as she walked me out of the building, she offered me the position as a 2nd-grade teacher. She said, "We really need men in our building, and it's hard to get good people here!" I was encouraged, but I told her that I had two other interviews I still wanted to give a shot. She understood.

The third interview was on Wednesday at the same school system my kids were attending. They have three Elementary schools. The interview went really well, and the principal asked me to come back the following week on Monday and teach a lesson to some of the teachers. I agreed to the meeting but did tell her I already had an offer and one more interview the next day.

My last interview was on Thursday with McCordsville Elementary in the Mt. Vernon School system, the same day, Elwood was going to be voting to approve me at their board meeting. I really thought I was going to be taking the job in Elwood, so I went into the interview very relaxed. My wife and I had talked through my stump speech many times and after a short meeting with Dan Denbow, the Principal who had founded the school ten years earlier and was retiring, and the new Principal, Stephanie Miller, and a few other teachers they asked me the key question. Why should we hire you? I said, "If you are looking for someone who is young and up on all the latest trends in education, then I am not the right person for you. But if you are looking for a man with integrity who can be a role model for young students, someone who has a lot of life experience to bring to the table with parents, is positive and who is a fast learner, then hire me!" I honestly said it with conviction and at the same time thinking I'm probably not what they are looking for. They thanked me and asked if I had any other questions, and I felt I needed to at least tell them that I was being approved at a meeting that night for another position. And then Dan asked me, "Are you planning to take the job if they approve you?" I paused for a moment, thinking if I say yes they will probably just move on. I said, yes!

As I walked out, I called my wife while I was driving out of the parking lot and told her it went as well as any interview all week, but that when I told them I had another offer and said I was going to take it, I felt like they will go another direction. Before my wife could respond, the principal called me and offered me the 5th-grade position. I couldn't believe it! I asked him if they would honor my master's degree in the pay scale since it was in theology instead of education. I was taking a pay cut in ½ from my salary after planting and leading a growing church for 13 years. He said he would ask the Superintendent and get back with me. Literally, within 2 minutes, while I was still on the phone with my wife, he called me back and said, the Superintendent actually answered the phone when he called the Admin office and said yes to my masters! How many Superintendents answer the phone? I asked him if he could give me a few hours to decide, and he said yes.

My wife was actually in Branson, Missouri, with our kids, her mom, and sister for a family trip. So we spent the next few hours talking through all the pros and cons. I felt like I needed to let Bev know before the meeting if I was not going to take the position so that she could nominate someone else. The key factors were proximity, McCordsville was only 15 minutes from our house, and the town was very stable economically and had strong parent involvement. Dyan and I both agreed that this job was a better fit for where I was emotionally in my recovery. So I called Bev and explained things to her, I felt bad because I believed in her and was thankful for her offer, she understood my decision. Then I called Dan back, and he was ecstatic!

I was excited, relieved, and scared to death all at the same time! I called my sister, Tish, who is one of the best middle school teachers around. She was so excited; I asked her if she would come out and help me set up my room, she and my sister Cheryl were a huge help to me! One of the other people I am indebted to is Jeannine Carder. She was a 2nd-grade teacher at McCordsville (MES), and from the first day I came in to get things ready, she took me under her wing! Even though I wasn't the new 2nd-grade teacher, they had a 2nd and 5th-grade position open when I interviewed; she was pushing for me to come to 2nd grade. She gave me a bunch of resources, taught me how to use the copier, and believed in me! We just connected! She reminded me of my sister, and she also started teaching later in life like myself.

My first semester was rough; I felt like I was just one day ahead of the students each day. I was still struggling with depression and hadn't yet accepted my new life working outside of ministry. Then I grabbed coffee with the former principal Dan Denbow, who called me to see how I was doing a few months into it. He asked me if I liked it and how it was going. I was honest with him about my struggle; then, he shared a few things with me that helped me realize what God was up to! So here's the part that I hope helps you see how God is always working ahead of us when we have no idea!

I asked Dan, 'Why did you hire me?" He then told me he got a phone call the week before the interviews by a guy named Tom Warmke. Tom told him you really need to take a look at Fred; he is a former pastor and a really solid guy. After he hung up the phone, he said he had a stack of applications 2 foot high on his desk. Mine was somewhere in the middle. Dan told me that he was curious why a guy in his mid-forties, who was a former pastor, would go into teaching. So he searched through the stack and found my application and called me! But it gets better!

Dan then told me he was a pastor's kid, and that he led worship at his church and viewed his job as a principal as his calling! He viewed himself as a pastor to his school. It's the way he led his team and worked with kids and parents. He spoke with such clarity about how his faith was integral to his everyday job in the world. I needed to hear that message. It started to reshape my view of my calling. Before I started Northeast, I sensed God telling me to reach the whole Northeast side of Indy for Christ. It took cancer and stepping away from my church to see that God had a much bigger picture than I did of my calling! I'll share more about this paradigm shift later.

Then Dan said it! Do you want to know the real reason why we hired you? I wanted someone to pass the spiritual leadership torch to for the school. I'll be honest; I didn't see it at first. But over time, I started to realize my new role! People would ask me spiritual questions. Most people looked at me like a pastor, and many parents were drawn to my story of being a former pastor and cancer survivor.

Then it happened, I finally pulled out of my depression over Christmas break a few months later. We had two weeks off and then there was a huge blizzard where we were buried with snow and ended up being off another full week. It was during that week when something finally clicked for me! I was honestly dreading going back, and one day I remember just thinking to myself, I am tired of feeling this way, I don't want to feel like I've failed God and everyone and like there is no hope for a better future anymore. So I just decided that I was going to be happy! I allowed myself to believe that I was forgiven, loved, and that God did still have BIG plans for my life. And that began a journey of me being able to start to learn to enjoy every day and look for how God was working in every part of my life! I went back to school and had a whole different mindset. I started to feel confident, have fun again. I began to get creative ideas of how to teach in fresh ways.

The next year, my Principal needed a teacher to move to 4th grade, and she thought it would be a good move for me, with another male teacher. His name is Chad Wimmenauer. It was really nice to have another guy on my team! We connected quickly, both being former athletes.

As I began to enjoy teaching, I started trying new ideas. One of the ideas I had was around a unit teaching business and economic growth for Indiana history. Our Social Studies curriculum had a one-page worksheet about developing a business plan. So I decided to let the students experience what it was like to become an Entrepreneur, what better way to learn these principles than having fun creating their own invention! Our family loved watching Shark Tank in the evenings. So I decided to create a Shark Tank Unit and Simulation Event.

I invited a few business friends of mine to be Guest Sharks in my room and even skyped in one of my Entrepreneurial friends Ozzie Kalil, who lived in Dallas, Texas! The kids had a lot of fun talking with him! The kids got so into it that I had to make them stop working on their business plan and product so they would do other work. I asked Chad if he wanted to also be a guest shark as another teacher and he fell in love with it! He ate up playing the Mr. Wonderful role!

The next year we decided to make it an entire 4th-grade unit. We created materials for every subject. We had over 63 Indiana Standards covered from Math to Writing, Presentation Skills, the Scientific Method, and more. Students had to put together their own promo video, and I brought in real Sharks, owners of multimillion-dollar companies. The Indiana

Superintendent of Schools, Glenda Ritz, even came to our production. I contacted all of the TV Sharks and invited them to participate, and Mark Cuban emailed me back from his phone, wishing us the best!

We did all of it in the gym with lights, cameras, and a board room setting. Our Art Teacher, Terry Trowbridge and Tech Director Jonathan Hendrix spent countless hours putting together our Shark Tank promo of how our teacher sharks became multimillionaires. It was a ton of work, but to see the students competing and so excited was incredible. The energy in the room with 600 students and parents was electric!

Chad ran all of our rehearsals and just owned it! One of the most rewarding moments from this experience was when Chad said to me after the event, "You've helped reignite my passion for teaching and upping my game creatively!" Wow! What a gift to be able to inspire others to live up to their full God-given potential!

The next year Chad actually took over the entire program, since I took a year off to try a business start-up with a friend. I came back to watch the event, and it was so rewarding to see other people owning it and taking it and running with it to make it even better! The next year I brought Shark Tank to one of the other Elementary Schools at Mt. Vernon with the help of a fellow teacher Lydgia Quinn Parker who caught the vision right away and helped add some new materials to the process, and I was able to raise

$5,000 to bring in Moziah Bridges from Mow's Bows. If you don't know Moziah Bridges, he appeared on Shark Tank when he was just 13 years old. Daymond John chose to mentor him, and he now runs a million-dollar company that makes designer bow ties. So he came to be our guest shark at the age of 18! This was a real treat for the kids! You talk about giving kids a vision of what they can do!

As my confidence grew, God began to show me other ways He wanted to use my life that were even more rewarding than anything I had done before! I now run a painting business that I love developing and growing with a vision to change people's lives by the way we treat them! I am a speaker, trainer, and coach with the John Maxwell Team, which is an incredible organization that helps add value to people's lives by envisioning people to live out their dreams! I have always been a student of John Maxwell through his books, and now I am enjoying writing so I can influence more people to unlock their full God-given potential so they can produce the results they want relationally and professionally!

I also run a University of Entrepreneurs where we train leaders on how to start and grow their own business! One of my mentors who has been an incredible encouragement in this area is Paul Martinelli. Paul leads the John Maxwell team and has grown four multi-million dollar companies. His faith is an integral part of everything he does from leading to speaking! He is one of the most positive Thinking Coaches and has such a genuine heart for God and people! When I went to my first International Maxwell Certification event, he spoke about how limiting thoughts hold us back and used science and faith to empower me to believe in my limitless potential. I had been thinking about writing books for a few years now, his influence on my life helped push me to believe in myself and the vision I see of helping people unlock their full God-given potential and to just start writing!

I hope you are picking up loud and clear that our recovery includes people that God intentionally puts in our path to help encourage and push and grow us to become the men and women we were made to be! I don't care how deep down you are right now. I know that God can heal your mind and grow you into a strong individual who has a clear vision for your life and that not only has hope but shares that hope with others who desperately need to hear a message of love!

Each year Pastor Dave from *iTown* writes me to share how God has worked and thanks me for what we did and we usually text and both of us believe that God is continuing the vision of Northeast and reaching the city of Indy for Christ and we are a part of that! I often think of the story of Abraham in the Bible, who was asked to sacrifice his son, who was God's promise of eternal blessing to humanity and Abraham decided to trust that God could resurrect his son. He ended up sparing his son, but God did resurrect his own son. I believe God had to get me to a place where I could let my son, *Northeast*, die so that he could resurrect an even bigger vision for my life!

It's not about me, and its way bigger than I ever imagined, now God can take me to places that I didn't see before! My cancer and businesses are taking me into the world in a way that has an even greater impact! You see, recovery is about so much more than ourselves! It's actually about getting past ourselves, outside of ourselves, and beyond ourselves, so God can truly use our lives to accomplish his purposes, which are way more important and last forever!

Do you see how small our visions are? Recovery is not the end goal; it's just the beginning my friends!

One of my favorite characters in the Bible is Joshua. He is the man who led God's people into the Promised Land and conquered dozens of Kingdoms and cities, taking new territory each day! A scripture I quote every day when I pray in the morning comes from the first chapter of Joshua. *"Do not be afraid or discouraged; the Lord, your God, is with you wherever you go. I've already given you the land, go possess it!"*[7] The scripture actually says I will give you wherever you put your foot! Joshua was a young man when God raised up Moses to deliver his people from 400 years of bondage. He was one of 12 spies Moses sent into the Promised Land to see if they should conquer it and he and Caleb were the only two who believed God could help them overcome the giants in the land. The other ten were filled with fear and convinced the rest of God's people that it was not possible. So the Israelites spent 40 years wandering in the desert until that generation died. Joshua waited for 40 years! He kept believing! And God used him to lead his people into a new land of promise! I believe God has already given you a future full of hope and promise and blessing; it's up to you to believe it and then go possess it!

ROUND 7: RELATIONAL HITS

I think this is one of the most important chapters of this book, that's why I had my wife write it. She was a rock for me, and it cost her a lot! The toll that a spouse or family caregiver goes through is just as difficult as the patient's battle, but we don't talk about it! Many marriages fail when a spouse or child goes through a major illness. It is very emotionally draining to watch a loved one go through physical and mental pain, and often it leaves family members feeling bad that they have some resentment inside to work through.

After I finally recovered from my depression, my wife was worn out! She shouldered all the emotional and financial responsibility and took care of the kids and managed all communication with our extended family, which was very concerned. She needed time to recover. It took some time for us to reconnect emotionally because of everything she also had to go through. This can be a very lonely time for couples and families.

This book was written about a season of my life when I was not able to be the man I wanted to be for my wife, and she shouldered it all for me and our family! I am incredibly thankful for the devotion my wife showed me while I battled depression and having to start over in my career while recovering from my cancer treatments.

You will quickly notice that this book is really all about our mindset. Because of my experience, I have resolved in my heart and mind that I will work diligently every day to live to my full God given potential so I fulfill my purpose, and so I am able to be the man my wife needs me to be for her! She deserves it! And so does God! And that all starts in my mind!

So I'm going to let my wife speak to this reality knowing that she will have a lot of wisdom to help guide your family through the healing process of all the hits families take when a loved one battles a serious illness. Not only is Dyan my best friend and the royal Queen of our family (her middle name is Esther, who was a queen) she is one of the most gifted professional counselors in her field! Dyan helps families every day as a school counselor, and she has guided our family with those skills over the years. So you are blessed to be learning from her! I will turn the rest of this chapter over to her.

I still remember exactly where I was sitting when Fred said he had something to share with me. We were on a dinner date at Houlihan's Restaurant. I quickly began to think through several possibilities of what Fred wanted to tell me - maybe a new idea/goal for our marriage and family or a change in our finances. I would never have guessed Fred would say he had cancer!

When he said the words, "I have cancer," I was in complete shock, and I immediately lost my appetite for dinner. It seemed so strange, but I did not cry right away; I felt shaken inside and the seriousness of what was to come in our lives. Throughout that first week, after Fred shared the news, I was in denial. It didn't seem real, as if it were a bad dream! Then, my sister, Suzi, called to tell me her cancer returned in her right breast for a second time. Immediately my mind flooded with the memories of Suzi's previous cancer treatment ... the sickness, the emotions, losing her hair, surgeries, fears, anxiety, etc. Ugh!

I remember crying out to God, "What in the world is happening? My husband and my sister both have cancer at the same time! I know your word says you won't give us more than we can handle, but I don't think I can endure all this at once!"
My sense of security was deeply shaken, but my brain and body immediately went into "mother mode" or protection mode. With all of the uncertainties and changes, I was going to be the rock of the family that kept everything running as normal as possible! This meant I did not feel a lot of emotion.

I was the family caregiver - spending my time and energy cooking meals; driving the kids to school, practice, and activities; making sure Fred scheduled his surgeries and dr. appointments; and reassuring the kids that their Dad was going to be just fine. I tried to keep our daily routines the same. Fred and I both felt it was important to not burden our kids with the stress and pressure of his cancer diagnosis.

Together, we told the kids about the cancer but shared it in a very positive manner. We explained Fred would have surgeries and treatment to ensure the cancer was removed and all cells killed. We let them ask questions at any point of the process.

At that time, we chose not to talk to them about the % chance of reoccurrence, possibility of the cancer spreading to other parts of the body, side effects from treatment, etc. We tried our best to give them an honest but age-appropriate understanding of what was happening with their dad. I was determined to be the "rock" or "constant" in the midst of all that was happening.

I also tried to be an encourager to Suzi during this time. I couldn't physically be with her, but I tried to call her regularly on the phone just to listen, share a timely scripture, and speak positive, hope-filled words to her. Again, it was my "protection mode" emerging wanting to protect my sister from negative thoughts and fears. As I look back, I don't think I could have managed this time of my life with hope and steadfastness without a deeply rooted faith in God through His Word and His promises in scripture.

It's so interesting to look back and see ways God had worked in my life when it made no sense at that particular time. Two years before Fred and Suzi's cancer, I graduated with my Masters in School Counseling. I didn't realize what my ideal career or job would be until I was in my late 20's - counseling in a school setting! It took me five years to complete 48 credit hours (equivalent to 2 years full-time).

During those five years of grad school, I overcame sickness, raising three kids, being in full-time ministry, and the death of my father. Needless to say, I was so excited to be finished with school and ready to get a full-time job doing what I love! Two years later and 30 interviews later, I finally found a school counselor position!

I prayed every day for God to open up a job so I could help our family financially. I couldn't understand why God was silent in answering those prayers, and nothing happened for two years. What I didn't realize at the time was God strengthening me, giving me much needed rest, teaching me to trust Him with every part of my life, and growing me close to His heart.

After losing my dad, I felt a void in my life of what a dad offers to his daughter - security, unconditional love and acceptance, and believing I can do anything I set my mind too. During this period, God filled the voids I felt from the loss of my dad. God was my solid, secure rock to stand on! God showered me with His love and held me in His arms close to his side. I experienced that love and acceptance once again! There is no price tag I can put on those two years of my life! They are worth far more to me than any amount of money. To this day, I am so thankful God gave me the gift of time, rest, quiet, and abundant love during those two years! They anchored me for what was about to come!!

I worked this new job for about six weeks before Fred was diagnosed with cancer. I was still getting used to working full-time along with managing a home, kid's activities, and church activities. It was definitely a transition time from my previous 14 years as a stay at home, mom! I loved my new job, but it was emotionally, mentally, and physically exhausting. The school I worked at had many children attending in poverty. Daily, I worked with kids displaying severe behaviors, emotional distress, abuse, and many physical needs. It was a stressful job but very rewarding to try each day to make a difference in these kids' lives.

My days were long as I drove thirty minutes each way to and from school. Once we discovered Fred's cancer, I felt extremely thankful for my job. The school health insurance for my whole family started three weeks before Fred was diagnosed with cancer! That saved our family over $100,000 in medical expenses alone plus providing income! I also made a very good friend, Mary Ann, who was my sounding board, a huge encourager, and a life-line for me during some very difficult days. Mary Ann was the School Nurse, and most days, we worked closely together with the children at school. We had many interesting experiences with students that led us to laughter and sometimes tears. Mary Ann was about 20 years older than me; she was a wise, calm, and caring presence in my life that I so needed. Mary Ann retired the year after Fred's cancer and to this day, I thank the Lord for bringing Mary Ann into my life at that exact time!

As I look back now, I see how beneficial it was for me to be in the work routine, staying busy, and keeping my mind occupied on my work instead of wondering about Fred's cancer. My days were full and busy, so when my head hit the pillow at night, I fell asleep quickly. I chose not to look up information about Fred or Suzi's cancer online. I didn't feel it would produce positive thoughts or feelings and questioned the accuracy of information from the internet.

I told myself I would listen and ask questions to the professionals; the dermatologist, surgeon, and oncologist. I read my Bible every day and wrote down specific promises from God in scripture that I would read over and over. I strategically placed them around my house and on my desk at work, so I was surrounded by God's words. I also used my 30-minute commute to worship. Thank goodness I was alone in the car because I would really "belt it out" and sing with all my heart to the Lord. It was a great time of surrender and being filled with God's amazing love. Those were excellent choices for me; it helped keep my thoughts positive and hope-filled instead of reading information and feeling fear, anxiety, or worry.

I remember feeling my stress levels rise as each day went by. At work, I experienced young kids hit, kick, and bite me. I also had to chase down our regular "runners" who would try to run out the door during the school day. Most days, I would leave work feeling very stressed. Then, I would come home to Fred, and the kids' needs and my stress level just continued to increase. I thought to myself, "How can I do this for days, months, or even a year?" Whenever I thought about managing work, home, Fred's health, the kids, Suzi's situation, and our church, I quickly became overwhelmed.

If I thought about the long process for Fred and Suzi of surgeries and cancer treatment, I felt overwhelmed. If I thought about the logistics of managing all the kids' schedules, needs, and activities, I felt overwhelmed. If I thought about all of the chores that needed to be done at home, I felt overwhelmed. The stress would quickly turn to anxiety that would flood my mind and heart, and it made me feel like there was no way I could do it all – I felt hopeless!

Then, one day, while reading my Bible, God made an important truth clear to me that I was not following: THINK ABOUT ONLY ONE DAY AT A TIME! When I thought about what I needed to do today, I could manage it! I would tell myself, "I can do today! Just one day! I can do this!" But, when I thought about the big picture and everything I needed to do in the coming days or months, I was filled with anxiety and felt like I couldn't do it. It helped me to stay focused on the present and not think back about the past or worry about the future. It felt doable for me to think about just one day. This was huge to learn, and it was my saving grace mentally, emotionally, and physically during many rough days!!

Living life one day at a time is a biblical concept. In Luke 11:3, Jesus states, *"Give us this day our daily bread."* This statement is within the Lord's Prayer, and Jesus is asking for the nourishment or daily bread he needs just for that day only. It refers back to the Israelites after crossing the Red Sea and reaching the desert. The Israelites began to complain to Moses because they were starving. God tells Moses, *"I will rain down bread from heaven for you. The people are to go out each day and gather enough for that day. In this way, I will test them and see if they will follow my instructions"*[8] At the end of the chapter, it states, *"The Israelites ate manna for forty years; until they came to a land that was settled".*[9] This passage still blows me away. God taught the Israelites to think about and live only one day at a time for forty years!!!! He provided for their daily needs for 14,600 days!!! Wow!

Another example is found in Luke 12:24, *"Consider the ravens: They do not sow or reap, they have no storeroom or barn: yet God feeds them."* Just thinking about the birds of the air reminds me how they live one day at a time. God provides for their needs each day!!

As I look back, walking through cancer with a close loved-one is a grieving process. I went through the stages of grief after discovering both Fred and Suzi had cancer. It wasn't that I felt either of them were going to die; it was walking through the unknown, the uncertainties, the sickness, and the change in our family dynamic. There are five stages in the grief process: denial, bargaining, anger, sadness, and acceptance. Right after hearing the news, I experienced both the denial and bargaining stages. It just didn't seem real. I remember asking myself repeatedly, "Was this just a bad dream, or is it actually happening?" but I quickly found myself bargaining with God. I would do just about anything if He healed Fred and Suzi! For me, the anger and sadness did not set in for a while. Again, I was in that protection mode, and I didn't allow myself to feel much emotion at the beginning. Good or bad, I felt as if my emotions were on autopilot for a while in order to maintain our family. I will say the emotions of sadness and anger came out in full force; it was later in the process when they hit!!

I think the first time I felt anger in this process was when Fred and I had differing opinions about taking medication during treatment. We had an in-depth discussion and came to the conclusion we had opposite views. I told Fred it was his body, so ultimately, it was his decision, and I would support him no matter what he decided!

So how do you support someone you love through a difficult time when you disagree with a decision he/she makes? As you are about to read, I was taken by surprise by my emotions of the coming days of Fred's depression. As Fred's side effects began, I became angry inside and found myself contributing it to his previous decision with the medication. I realized the anger inside my heart made it difficult for me to be caring and compassionate, which he so desperately needed from me at that time. When I realized what was happening inside of me, I had to stop myself and change my focus. I told myself, "That is enough! I have to let go of the past." Part of this process involved changing the way I thought about the situation. Instead of thinking, "If only Fred would have..." I began to tell myself, "I am Fred's wife; I love him with all my heart! I made a vow on our wedding day to love and care for him in sickness and in health, for better or for worse, until death do us part!" It was a complete change of attitude from a victim mindset to a proactive approach, focusing on my part and what I can do! This made a huge difference and helped me to truly love him through a very difficult time!

During Fred's treatments, I also felt anger directly toward the *Interferon* for what it was doing to Fred's body, physically, emotionally, and mentally. There was nothing I could do to stop or change what was happening to Fred. Often, I felt helpless, and that increased my frustration.

At the same time, I experienced deep sadness when I saw the intensity of Fred's struggle. His personality, anxiety level, and ability to think/process information had completely changed! For a time, he didn't eat or sleep and was continually in a state of panic. My heart felt so broken for him! I remember feeling so solemn during that time.

Our extended family and close friends were a huge support and encouragement for me during Fred's severe reaction to *Interferon*. They prayed, encouraged, helped around the house, drove Fred to appointments, and stayed with Fred while I went to work. It breathed life into me just to have that support and help! Outside of family and close friends, I did not share the specifics during this time with others. I felt strongly it was important to protect Fred and let him share his experience at his choosing.

As time passed, Fred began to heal. He had a wonderful psychiatrist that worked closely with him for many months. He also received therapy in groups and individually. As he began to feel better and recover physically, emotionally, and mentally, I began to feel weak and exhausted. It seemed so strange to me that my husband's health was tremendously improving, but I lost my energy, joy, and desire to do activities and be with people. Actually, it is a common phenomenon called the "Let Down Effect." This is when a person's body gets sick physically, emotionally, or mentally after sustaining a long period of stress or trauma.

Fred was ready to go - gaining energy, stamina, and the desire to be with people. On the other hand, my body was letting down from the intensity of stress I carried for months - exhausted, weak, not able to think or plan any activities, and desiring to be alone. I did the "essentials" of work and took care of my family, and that was it. I didn't serve at church or in the community, and I didn't spend time with friends. I didn't have enough strength or energy.

This Let Down Effect lasted for about a year. Fred and I learned to navigate the challenges of our differing needs in our marriage relationship at that time and continued to grow ourselves in learning to love and serve each other. During this year, the reality of everything that happened with the cancer set in, and as I processed through this in my mind, I had to come to a place of acceptance. Fred was not completely back to himself in every aspect of his central nervous system, cognition, and strength. I remember coming to the point that I accepted this new state of Fred's physical, emotional, and mental health. He had greatly improved from the previous months, and I was so thankful he was alive. I no longer wondered if his mind was ever going to return to the "old Fred." I accepted the cancer, the treatment, and his current state. That was freeing for me - no more wondering or wishing. I believe that was part of my healing during the Let Down Effect.

I look back now and see so many AMAZING ways God sustained me, grew me, loved me, and provided for our family. Those were very difficult days, but I see a greater good and purpose in it now. My marriage is stronger and closer now than it was before the cancer.

Each day has a different meaning now - I treasure who I am with and what I am doing each day! My faith grew tremendously through this experience. I no longer fear sickness, job loss, and difficult times because God is always with me and carries me through my trials every step of the way! I can't tell you how many times I have encouraged someone else with the idea of living life one day at a time. It's more than I can count. I will continue to share that amazing truth from God's Word for the rest of my life; it still impacts me. To sum it up, Fred's cancer experience changed my perspective in so many ways! I am truly thankful each day for every blessing from God - big and small!

SECTION THREE

INSPIRATION
AND TRUTH
FROM A FRIEND

FREDTALK:
INSPIRATION & TRUTH FROM A FRIEND

I have my kids to thank for Fred Talk! My wife and I have a special relationship with our kids. We often just look at each other and say we are so blessed to have the kids we do! So here's how Fred Talk started:

I hated my name growing up. Fred, it's an older person's name, or a cartoon caveman - Fred Flintstone! I had my share of being made fun of! Even as I became an adult and planted a church in my 30's when people would come to visit, they would tell me that they thought the pastor would be like 80 years old! Depending on the era of people you talk to, I am known by different names! Growing up, it was Freddie! For my grandpa it was Freddie the Freeloader! In high school, my nickname was Cec, short for my middle name, Cecil. In college, my roommate and one of my best men at my wedding, Keith Gordon, called me Fredwire, Gordo still calls me that to this day!

Here's one thing I've learned over life; there is something special about a name! I love to give people nicknames, helps me remember their name, and makes a special bond! In fact, I study names a lot; I like to know the meaning behind them, Dyan and I frequently talk to our kids about the meaning of their names. And I call her my Celestial Queen, that's what Dyan Esther means. And what does Fredrick mean? Peaceful Ruler! That fits me pretty well! I like to enjoy people and have influence to help people become all that God made them to be!

My kids are famous for saying mom and dad like to have "talks." They love to dramatize how they got sucked into our bedroom for a serious closed-door talk and barely made it out alive! My oldest son, Seth, is hilarious with impersonations! He always keeps us laughing, and he even feels safe to make fun of mom and dad! Many nights at the dinner table on special occasions with our grown kids he will start talking about how mom and dad would tell him we need to talk with you, and then embellishes this grand story that has us all laughing and mom saying I don't do that, which makes us all laugh even more!

Every kid thinks their parents are out of date! I remember having fun with my older sister Tish imitating our parents and having secret looks and words that we used to make us laugh! My kids also love to take pictures and little videos of me and send them to their friends with some funny tag line. Often it's me working out to my music, either 80's rock or a current rap song from a movie; other times its just random photos. Most of their friends know me on an inside friend level. So when they say hi Fred there's usually a big grin or chuckle behind it. They have a lot of fun with this! I used to take myself too seriously; my kids and their friends have helped me not to take things so personally! If my Fredness can endear them to me, I'll use it!

I'm famous for having little talks with their friends. Dyan and I love connecting with our kids and their friends, and we love having them over at our house. We knew what they were doing, gave them freedom but also were able to have a read on their friends and love on them and influence them! Many of them called Dyan mom and vacation with us and are a part of our family.

Whenever I would come home and see our kids' friends, I would always say, "Hey, Hey! … Guys, how you doing?" with a big smile. This became legendary! They would repeat it back with gusto! Then they knew I was going to plop down on the couch and chat for a while and always add some positive, inspirational faith to whatever they were telling me about! Then some advice was always mixed in, to where they just came to expect some Fred Talk! I am also famous for sending these through text messages!

My kids' friends would see me and say, "Hey Fred, so what's up?" They would share with me about stuff at school or sports or life, and I would usually ask a question as my lead into my Fred Talk! Something like you do know why that's happening, don't you? Or, you do know what makes champions? And my youngest son Luke always pipes up and says I know what you're going to say, dad, faith, you have to believe! You believe I can do anything! He's right! We set the limits, not God!

I love it when the kids ask me questions about life; it's my open door to speak life and truth into them! See, I have a few foundational beliefs that propel me to take advantage of every opportunity to speak grace and truth into people's lives!

First, I believe with my core in the power of words to give life or death. God says his word never returns empty; it always does what he wants it to do! It's how he created life. It's how we grow faith. Words are powerful, my friends! And I also know we get way too much death thrown at us every day! We start to believe that crap and replay it in our heads. So I feel a deep calling to give some Fred Talk every chance I get!

So when I started labeling my inspirational text's Fred Talk, then I started creating short 2 minute videos of Fred Talk. And the kids would say, I saw your Fred Talk on Twitter or Facebook. Some teens have even shown them to their high school class when they have to teach motivational lessons. So that's when I had my daughter Chelsea create my website **Fred-Talk.com**. She convinced me to use a Bitmoji as my image to make it playful and fun! Since my kids are getting older, I thought I'll just share this with the world! So this section of the book is just some Fred Talk just between you and me as friends! It's laced with lots of positive inspiration and truth. Jesus never spoke just grace or just truth; it was always a mix of both!

Nobody likes to admit weakness! I like to win and feel strong and capable. I hate feeling like I've let people down or failed to live up to what I know God wants for my life. I struggled with feeling less than as a husband and father when I was going through my depression and between careers not providing well for my family. I second-guessed myself, wondering if I wasn't able to start over with a new career. I usually love life, but I've thrown way too many pity parties in my life. And my setbacks with cancer and the depression from the treatment and then the insecurities from feeling like I had failed in my calling have taught me some things about myself that I needed to learn.

So I'm going to just share from my heart some things I've had to grow in that have made me stronger and has helped me navigate life better!

Remember my name is Fred, and I'm your friend!

LESSON 1: GET OVER YOURSELF

Growing up, I was always the smallest kid, and I was very sensitive. These two qualities do not usually fit with football! But I loved football, even at 55lbs in 5th grade! I grew up in northeast Ohio, Stark County, Pro Football Hall of Fame, High School powerhouses like Massillon where Paul Brown won state every year, then went on to coach at Ohio State, and then the NFL with the Browns and the Bengals.

I started playing tackle football in 1st grade, I didn't weigh much more than the ball, but I dreamed of playing in the NFL! Back in the 70's the staple drill was bull in the ring, where one person was in the middle, and everyone else took a turn at hitting that person as hard as they could, builds toughness, I hated it! I liked to hit, but I had no chance against guys two and three times my size.

I always loved the strategy side of the sport. As a coach, I love scheming how to take advantage of the defense's weaknesses and position the right players in their best role to score as many touchdowns possible. Even though I wasn't able to lift as much as most guys, I was scrappy, and I had worked hard all summer going into my last year of High School. I played backup wide receiver and defensive back my senior year and was the starting punter and kicker at a whopping 125lbs. We had a really strong program and went undefeated my senior year. We were ranked #1 in the State!

Our running back, Leon Powell, was First-Team All-State and had rushed for over 2,000 yards in 10 games! We were a small town and had played some bigger cities that year. Our only close game was against Canton South where my dad, our team chaplain, broke three ribs when a player ran into him on the sidelines, he had to be taken to the hospital, and we won by one point. Their kicker missed an extra point, and I didn't! We finally made the playoffs for the first time in our school's history. In Ohio Football you have to earn your way into the playoffs.

We ended up playing horrible, including three fumbles, but we still had a chance to win at the end. The game was tied, and I was set up for a 35-yard field goal. I'll never forget what my teammate, Doug Hayes, said to me in the huddle, "Make this, and we'll love you forever!" And if I miss? I was nervous; we had a field goal attempt that was blocked earlier in the game. I kicked it and had plenty of distance, but it started to drift off to the left and hit the upright! I thought, no way! But then it went in! We thought we had won! But then we heard a whistle and saw a flag; the ref said someone had jumped offside, so we had to back it up 5 yards and try again from 40 yards out.

Now all I was focused on was getting it straight. When I kicked it, it was dead on, right down the middle. It just hung in the air and ended up falling literally inches short! We fumbled again in OT and ended up losing. I cried for a long time in the locker room. That was my last game ever in High School football. It sucks when you have an opportunity to succeed, to help your team win and you failed. Life has a way of making us face feelings of doubt, or like we are a loser, people can contribute to it also.

Here's what I've learned, most people that criticize you do it out of fear, so they feel better about themselves. And no failure is the end unless you choose to believe that you are a failure. My best growth comes from mistakes and failures. I've learned there is a seed of success in every failure if you will look for it and choose to see it as an opportunity to learn and grow from it, you will be ready next time. Successful people fail the most; they just never allow themselves to personalize it and never quit. This takes faith! Faith in yourself!

Listen, you can believe in God, but if you don't believe in yourself, you will struggle your whole life. God wants you to be confident in who you are, not cocky, but willing to push through what others think or say or whatever you face and be who he created you to be! Insecurity reduces God to what you are comfortable with. If you want to do great things with your life, you can't limit yourself. You have to get past yourself because if you're going to do something great with your life, there will be a lot of doubters and challenges.

Well, I wasn't done with football! I still had more desire in me to play! So I went on to play college football at Anderson University. I wanted a chance to go to a new place and earn a starting position. I ended up being a three-year starter, led the team in receiving my senior year and that last play of College career was toward the end of a close game that was rainy and muddy. We had the ball on the 2-yard line. The coach called a swing route, I went in motion then swung to the outside and had my guy beat, the ball was thrown short, so I jumped inside of the defender and caught it on our 40-yard line. He fell, so it was just me and the free safety and 60 yards to go! I felt like I was as slow as molasses! But I ended up scoring a 98-yard touchdown! Set a school record that still stands almost 30 years later.

It's the only record in all of the years and sports I played I ever set, and it happened on my last play ever in football. The record isn't really what means so much to me; it's that it redeemed my last play of High School!

I can't tell you how many times I have gone back to this experience during difficult challenges in my life when I've felt insecure or weak; I remind myself that I am a strong finisher, God is not done yet! I am so grateful for the opportunity to play college ball, even at 145lbs! I was able to experience some really special things, like playing alongside Brad Lamb, who went pro and played for the Buffalo Bills in 3 of their 4 Super Bowls! I was invited to an NFL combine after my senior year and had a fun time with my Dad down in Louisville, KY, and I still have the shirt! There were other cool stadiums we played in, and just the experience with the guys was so fun! Then there are guys I've met since my playing days that I found out we played against each other like Chris Cochran who I ended up coaching little league against!

I am confident that you have your own story of times when you have failed and struggled with personalizing that failure. I don't care what you've done, how bad your situation is, God is not done with you!

I'm often reminded of the story of Moses, who constantly questioned himself and numerous times limited God by telling Him he stuttered and couldn't speak well. He even allowed his insecurities to cause him to blame others for his choices that ended up causing him to miss out on taking God's people into the Promised Land, which was God's plan for his life! Don't allow your insecurities to limit you from becoming who God wants you to be!

You must replace negative, limiting thoughts with life-giving truths about yourself! Get over yourself, quit throwing pity parties, they're no fun, and nobody ever comes to them! Have you figured that out yet? People aren't drawn to our negativity.

Remember, my name is Fred, and I'm your friend! If you really want to grow your faith in yourself, then take my online Faith Survey at **www.Fred-Talk.com.**

You will get a report ranking your faith in God, Yourself, and Others. Then dive into the resources I have to help you grow your faith! Contact me about being your Mindset Coach or invest in one of my online courses, come hear me speak live!

I love you enough to believe in you and challenge you! Create your own story of redemption! Believe it and live it!

LESSON 2: POSITIVITY ALWAYS WINS!

Life sucks sometimes. People complain a lot; I call them life-suckers; they just suck the life out of everyone and everything around them. The world fixates on negativity, and you know why don't you? It speaks to one of our deepest fears: scarcity.

Not having enough, whether it's money, love, time … Most people live their lives in fear and don't even realize it, because they were conditioned to believe in a scarcity mindset.

We are told DON'T 20x's more than do! That is probably a low estimate! We've all read research studies on how important it is to counter all the negative input with positive and how we tend to fixate on one negative comment out of five good ones. One study says that by the time we are adults we will have heard "No" or "Don't" or "You can't" 150,000 times vs. hearing "Yes," or "You can" 2,000 times.

One UCLA survey reported that the average one-year-old hears NO 400x's a day. At first, we think NO WAY! But think about how we correct toddlers full of energy, it usually comes in 3's, no, no, no! No, no, you can't … Words multiply quickly!

We are programmed from a young age with a scarcity mindset. Just think of some of the guiding principles we remember from growing up. Don't trust strangers. In fact, people have to earn your trust (a bias toward doubting) Money doesn't grow on trees. (shortage)

You better do well in school because if you don't go to college you can't get a good job. (Don't trust yourself, work for someone else) The majority of the messages we believe are negative and limiting.

So we spend most of our lives trying to get our share and protect it. As a pastor for over 20 years, I loved to talk about giving because you could see people squirm when you talk about a 10% tithe as a baseline starting point just to thank God for all of his abundant provision. If we really believe in God's abundance, then why does the average Christian only give 2-3%? Fear, scarcity, lack of faith. Remember, my name is Fred, and I'm your friend!

Jesus said it is better to give than receive. That is truth my friend, not just feel-good talk! And yes that applies to money as much as it does to love and time!

So to protect our money, we say things like, God cares more about your heart. Funny though, Jesus equated our handling of money as a picture of our heart. I hope this one paragraph gets you so convicted that the rest of your life you can't sleep without prioritizing giving to God and his work on this earth through the church to spread his message of the love of Jesus Christ to the world. Stop tipping God like you are doing something for him! He doesn't need your money, he wants your heart, and it's attached to your money. Start giving God your BEST first fruits and then live on what is leftover. God will see to it that you have more than you need!

After teaching on giving to my church back in the mid-2000s, I felt challenged to grow my giving beyond the tithe and other missional things we did above that. So I set a goal that giving would be our largest investment of money.

I say investment because it reminds me of the intentionality of how we use our resources rather than viewing it as just spending. Giving was behind our mortgage, car expenses, and food budget. After a few years of working at it, in 2010 giving climbed to 2nd, only behind food. I am a big eater, even when I was skin and bones I've always "slammed the chicken" as my good friend Steve Harris says! And my boys can slam the chicken!

Stevo is my financial advisor and was a Northeaster who had a heart for giving and always wondered if his financial gifts mattered as much as his service and he inspired me to grow in my giving! As a former college athlete Steve loves coming to watch, my boys play High School football! My oldest son Seth was a lineman in football and weighed 240lbs when he played! And Dyan is an amazing cook! If you come to dinner at the Bays', you will not go home disappointed! Plus, we've always had lots of extra kids at our house; we love to be the hang out place! So I was determined to grow our giving to be the top investment!

When I had to step away from Northeast, my salary cut in half as a starting teacher, we still continued to tithe 10%, but the amount was much less. This was discouraging because I love to give in ways that bless God's Kingdom work as much as I can! That first year when I wasn't working and trying insurance was very hard, Dyan shouldered our entire financial burden, and her mom was a tremendous help! My dear friend Doug Talley, from Indiana Ministries, helped me apply for a grant for pastors in transition! After getting back on our feet, and my painting business taking off, I was so grateful to see giving grow to our top budget expense in 2018. A lot of people have a love/hate relationship with money and do not see it as something spiritual. I found so much satisfaction when I did my taxes that year and was able to celebrate fulfilling that step! In fact, I knew I was going to hit my goal after the 1st year of my painting business, so I set my next, giving goal of one million dollars. I am so excited to see how God uses this next investment in what he is doing in the world!

I had also set another financial goal the year before stepping away from Northeast. I felt led to pay back Indiana Ministries the money they had invested in us as a start-up ten years earlier so they could plant more new churches that would reach people for Christ! After we dissolved Northeast, I still felt responsible for that step. So when God started blessing my painting business, I decided to begin giving back to Indiana Ministries out of my own personal income. I can't tell you how rewarding it is to bless the Kingdom in this way! I love talking with Doug each year to hear how God is expanding new works and to get to play a small part in that just fills me with joy!

When I started moving in the direction of speaking, coaching, and writing books, I was inspired by Pastor Rick Warren's talk at his church's 30-year celebration. He was asked why he thought God blessed his book to sell millions? He said, "I know exactly why because God knew what I would do with the money!"

Rick and his wife decided to reverse tithe when his book became a bestseller, they tithe 90% and live on 10%. Now before you say it, let me just stop you right now, no you wouldn't! Don't deceive yourself into thinking that you would give like that if you had millions of dollars. Jesus said, whoever is faithful with a little, will be faithful with a lot. Whoever is not faithful with a little, will not be faithful with a lot! That is the truth, my friend! Rick went on to explain that he didn't just jump from 10-90. For the first 25 years of his marriage and ministry each year they grew their giving percentage, 1%, 2%, 5% and more. When his book made millions, they were already tithing at 50%, so God knew their character, not their intentions, and that's a big difference!

After this talk, I wrestled for months with the impression that I should commit to giving 50% of all my new business ventures moving forward. I spent time talking with some older trusted pastors I respected. The last one I talked with said why commit to it, let your yes be yes and no be no. If God blesses, you give more. Sound advice! Then he said I had a chance to expand my business and decided not to because I didn't want to be in the world. And immediately I knew what I needed to do! I feel called to go into the business world and affect it for good! If I want to have influence to challenge wealthy business leaders to give generously to God's Kingdom work, then I need to set the example! Also, I want my heart to stay focused on what God is up to more than what I want. So I committed to tithing 50% of all my profits moving forward with my speaking, coaching, and writing. I know God is going to give me way more than I need and I'll get to that one million dollar goal a lot quicker! My wife is in charge of our Foundation, and we can't wait to meet all of the amazing leaders we work with see how God grows his agenda! Friends, it's a privilege to give abundantly, because God is the one who owns it all and shares it with us in the first place! You can't out-give God! He's got more reserves than we will ever need!

Positivity, optimism, generosity, faith, love always wins! Because God is on that side! He is an abundant blesser. There is no shortage. Positive qualities of thinking compound over time and are much more powerful than negativity. Do you know why? Because negative energy destroys; positive energy creates. It's death vs. life and life wins!

God's enemy, Satan is on the wrong side. Don't allow yourself to get deceived into believing a lie. Negativity never wins. Fear-based responses never last. God never makes you follow his ways. He loves you into a relationship. That builds loyalty and true safety and security!

This is why I always say; look for the seed of success in every difficult situation. It's in there. Stop looking for the negative; you'll find what you want to find. People have asked me my whole life, why are you so positive, why do you smile so much, how do you have so much energy? Some people think I have it easy; they say things like … you've got a good marriage, you have good kids, you're lucky. I've been called a dreamer and unrealistic so many times that I actually like it now.

I just laugh! Cancer, depression, major career change in my forties, starting three successful businesses and organizations, raising three kids to be strong independent God-fearing adults, actually being more in love after almost 30 years of marriage, publishing a book, … those things are all so easy! It's just been a cakewalk! I don't understand real problems. HaHaHa! Whose the dreamer? Who's unrealistic? And friends, my best is yet to come! The mountains I'm going to move with my faith are way bigger than the ones I just listed!

You see my friend; if you choose a daily workout diet of faith and positivity, you're muscles grow stronger and stronger. Your confidence in yourself gets more resolved deep down in your soul because you realize that God is an abundant loving Father, and it's in our DNA to be like our dad! And our big brother already removed the limitations of our sins and set us free to become who we were created to be! The more you discipline yourself to study the truth and focus on setting your mind right, the more you get to know the true character of our Lord's goodness. He alone is good. He alone is God. He will never forsake you! You are not alone! You have already won! Our job is simply to live by faith and walk into the promises God already prepared for us! Are you beginning to see why I am convinced with crystal clarity that positivity wins?

So let me share a little secret with you. Do you know where positivity comes from? What is its source? The scriptures teach that everything that is good and perfect comes from above. Don't deceive yourself into thinking that we are the source of life and positivity. I could write an entire book detailing this truth, but that book has already been written!

People don't have to acknowledge that God is the source of all that is positive for it to be true, my friends. If you're not sure about the source of all that is good in your life, and if we are our own source, then we are giving ourselves credit for creating something we did not create. When I stand before my maker my only response will be thank you for all you did for me; I am choosing to spend my life stewarding the gifts God has given me to glorify him and accomplish his purpose. Because it's the least I can do, he traded his life for death, so we could be made right! That is a God I can trust and want to serve! We win!

I have created a Faith Survey that you can take online in five minutes that will help you see where you at in your faith in God, yourself, and others. Just go to

www.Fred-Talk.com and click the link Faith Survey. You will get a report emailed to you.

This will help you see where you are at right now in each area and then give you some steps you can take to tangibly grow your faith in each area. You do know that positivity is just another word for faith, don't you? A belief in something you can't see that you believe is good! It's a mindset. It's a Belief System. And those of you who think that's just a bunch of BS, oh you of little faith! Doubt never wins! Have faith!

LESSON 3: BUILD DISCIPLINES

I am not proud to say that for the first 30 years of my life, I was sporadic with prayer and Bible study. I did not see the value in memorizing scriptures, and I didn't understand the power of the spoken word, and I was a youth pastor! When we planted Northeast in 1999, I made some commitments to build personal disciplines that would grow my relationship with my Creator. I started using a format to pray, that enabled me not to get distracted. I read the Bible at a set time each day and memorized a handful of scriptures that spoke to me and started fasting every Monday to remind myself that what we see doesn't sustain us as much as what we don't see.

When my cancer hit, and I had to work through the depression from my treatments, having a dozen years of practice in these disciplines, paid off with a big ROI (Return on Investment). Learning how to pray and grow your faith in God and His truth has a compounding effect over time! It's hard to draw on what you don't have.

I liken it to investing. If you spend all of the money you make as you make it when big expenses come you won't have anything to draw from. But if you consistently invest money and live on less, you will have reserves!

The same is true in relationships! Always work to build reserves every day with your spouse and kids and those you work closely with, it pays huge dividends when you need to make a withdrawal!

So I'm just going to walk you through the format I use and what a day looks like for me praying. It took me a while to find my own personal style of relating to God. I tried sitting quietly. I tried kneeling. I tried closing my eyes, none of those things ever worked for me. I'm an activist; my mind quickly jumps if I'm not doing something. So I decided to run with that!

I discovered that I prayed best when I either took walks, was driving in the car, working out, journaling or listening to songs that moved my spirit (they aren't all worship songs, there is no such thing as Christian songs, since a Christian is not an adjective, some songs talk about God some don't. I have no problem bringing thoughts of God into music, movies, or other media or even interactions with people).

I try to spend 5-10 minutes every morning before I leave for work to read a passage in the scripture. I don't try to read a ton. I read a short section and underline, write my thoughts on the page, read the notes in my study Bible, and then often find myself thinking about that story or truth throughout my day.

On the weekend or sometimes a weeknight when I'm not really busy, I may sit down for an hour and read and study more. This is a habit. Often I take my Bible to work and will read it during breaks. It's my favorite book to read, and I read a lot of books.

A little Fred Talk for a minute about reading books: I didn't read a book until I was in my late 20's! I hated to read growing up! I couldn't remember what I would read on a page. I would have to read it three times just to get a handle on it. Teachers wanted to put me on medication when I was little because I was a ball of energy.

I would be labeled lots of things today! ADD, ADHD, slow reader, squirrelly! Let me speak as an educator (I've taught Elementary school for five years) and as a business owner for a minute. Most people who are naturally high energy, creative, and visionary get easily bored and find most educational materials disinteresting and are wired to drive their own learning. I have found when you engage people in what they love and are passionate about they can focus for hours. I haven't changed in my energy level or getting easily bored, but I can concentrate longer than most people can manage. So the problem isn't the wiring!

The word educate comes from two Latin words *educare*, which means to train up or mold, like a child; and *educere*, meaning to draw out. Most institutions focus solely on the first meaning of pouring into or training. But our best and earliest learning happens from leading out! How do we learn to walk? We are not taught; we draw it out of us by trial and error. This is how the brain learns best; it engages our imagination and grows our self-confidence, rather than placing our worth and value on what standardized testing says is intelligence.

There is a reason why most of the wealthiest people have less education than the millions of people who work for them. The people who transformed our world on a mass level like Ben Franklin, John Rockefeller, Henry Ford, Walt Disney, Ted Turner, Richard Branson, Bill Gates, Steve Jobs, Mark Zuckerberg, (and the list goes on) all dropped out of school. Your best growth doesn't come from institutions. I'm not against education, I have a Master's Degree, but that knowledge did not help me succeed in relationships, business, and life.

I started loving reading when I found things I was interested in. And the people that I resonated best with, entrepreneurial leaders all said leaders are readers. So I started looking at what they read. It's called self-guided learning. We all naturally gravitate towards it. Then I started listening to books on tape and found, as long as the voice wasn't stoic, I was an auditory learner. I could retain most things I heard better than what I would read. Then as I got out into the world and was stepping out trying things, I learned that I am a kinesthetic learner! I learn by doing, moving, and trying things.

This was really empowering. I wondered for a long time why other people are so scared to try things and then realized that most people are programmed with something that tells them they must know how to do it first, so they don't fail. It's a fear mindset. Some people are wired to watch and study first before getting it. There is nothing wrong with this approach as long as it comes from a healthy abundance mindset that encourages trial and error rather than a scarcity mindset that views mistakes as bad and embarrassing, so avoid them, so you are safe.

I am a lifelong learner, just not through academia. There is a self-righteousness that many institutions and educators have that often looks down on people who don't learn the way they think is best. And this mindset, which is fear-based and controlling, is being taught to our kids and kids either believe the lies that you can't make something of yourself without a college education or they buck the system and are the trouble kids that decide to pave their own path. What if we had a system that was designed to draw out rather than try to stuff in?

We learn best when we think we discovered it! Nobody likes to be told what to do. The best educators, parents, leaders learn how to guide people into growth. That's why Jesus asked so many questions! He taught people how to think and let people wrestle with truths through self-discovery. He was always reframing perspectives!

Education is making strides in validating learning styles, but most standardized tests and training focuses on irrelevant intelligence and controlling mindsets rather than practical principles of growth laws that foster learning and empowering mindsets.

We're trained in life to prepare for the test, rather than being taught how to think. Then when we get in the real world, the rules change, and students don't feel prepared for their career or life. On top of that, they have a ton of debt! And the college system with tenure tends to reinforce this elitist attitude for many teachers. Some of the stories of things my kids have heard from teachers and had to deal with had nothing to do with preparing them for their career.

This is why I have started a business called the University of Entrepreneurs; it's a trade school for leaders who want to start their own business. We guide students through experiences of self-discovery and mindset. We help teach students how to think, not what to think. We encourage them to look within and believe that our potential is limitless if we can identify the limiting beliefs we have about ourselves and replace them with positive, life-giving thoughts!

We also partner entrepreneurs up with other seasoned business leaders for mentoring and expect that our students will add value to those leaders and companies! For more info about our approach and program visit **www.UofEntrepreneurs.com**

Ask the typical boy if they like school. What's your favorite subject? Recess, lunch, Physical Education! When I see teachers that "get it," the boys especially seem to have fun. They want to learn, and they have very few discipline problems. I have to say that MES, where I've worked, has a lot of teachers who get this, and the Principal, Stephanie, gets it and gives a lot of room for teachers to experiment.

Why did I spend time challenging our education system? Because it dramatically affects every aspect of our lives! And it's based on a fear mindset, a scarcity mindset. It limits the way God designed us to grow and learn!

We used to have Sunday School! We think the pastor is more spiritual because he's educated! These mindsets are not from God or scripture. So no wonder people say they are intimidated to read the Bible or feel like they don't know how to pray. Most people who go to church view it as a time to get poured into (educated, edified), but that is not the Biblical view we get from God! Jesus said we are the church, His Holy Spirit is in us, and we are to go out into the world and confidently know He is with us and will guide us in what to say. He has put his truth in our hearts and our conscience. The reason we come together to church is to bring our heart of praise for all God has done for us and to thank God and edify one another. Our belief system is faulty, so we expect the pastors to know how to guide us, we struggle with joy and success in relationships and handling parenting, our finances and knowing how to share our faith with our neighbors. So what is the answer?

Grow yourself! Stop expecting the church to grow your faith and self-confidence and your kids. Take personal responsibility for your own spiritual growth. Remember, my name is Fred, and I'm your friend! You can do this! You can figure it out! You have the Almighty God who created you and knows your strengths and weaknesses and has already planned out every single day of your life living inside of you if you are a believer in Jesus Christ! So what are you waiting for? Why are you giving away that power to someone else?

So let me break it down very simply for you so you can empower yourself to develop to your full God-given potential and come to know the ONE and ONLY TRUE POWERFUL GOD who says, with me, all things are possible for you! Let's learn how to pray and grow our faith!

As you read the Bible find passages that speak to your heart and help you grow confident and overcome insecurities. Don't get stuck on the passages that confuse you. Not all scripture will speak as profoundly to you as it does to someone else. That's OK! I'm not saying avoid the truths you don't like, I'm saying focus on the ones that speak loudest to your heart. It's God's way of showing us what he wants us to do in this life! Memorize those scriptures and say them over and over out loud to yourself. Claim the promises of God. I will share some of the favorites that I use every day in my prayer times!

So let's talk prayer for a few minutes. Prayer is just a conversation with God. We speak and listen. But we do it on his terms! This is foundational! You don't tell your creator how it is! It's fine to vent and be honest, but if your purpose of prayer is to get what you want and feel better about it, sorry, no parent wants to bless spoiled brats! But if my son comes to me with respect and genuinely wants a relationship with me, to spend time with me, I want to bless that type of attitude. Your posture is key!

Jesus was asked, "How should we pray?" He said, don't babble on like the hypocritical religious people do who pray so long in front of others that the food gets cold! HaHa, now that one is really funny! You can ask my wife and kids and friends when we eat my prayer is short; the focus is thanking God for the food and family, Amen! If you have to use mealtime to get your prayers in for everyone you're not praying enough on your own time. Jesus said, keep it short in public. Keep it simple; don't use big theological words. He's not impressed. If that stuff matters to you, then that's all the recognition and blessing you're going to get!

The prayers that move God's heart are in private! You're own time! He sees it! And people will know because you will have such a confidence and strength and peace that it's obvious you work out a lot more and are in really good spiritual shape.

Here are the words Jesus used. It's called the Lord's prayer. It's not the words, but the concepts that give us a frame to use. Surprisingly, I learned it during High School football, and it was not a Christian school, even though there is no such thing since a Christian is not an adjective, it's a person living for Christ! I didn't learn The Lord's Prayer in church. We prayed it every night before our games at midfield and then would yell, Kick-Ass! I just find that really funny! I love you, Lord, and forgive others, now let me go kill someone!   Actually, the end of the prayer that Jesus taught us to pray does have a kick-ass part, and I'll explain that in a minute. If you're an athlete, you'll love it! You can find the verses in Matthew 6:9-13, but I'm going to break it down into five parts:

Jesus said, pray like this:

1. Our Father in Heaven, hallowed be your name!
2. Your Kingdom come, your will be done, on earth as it is in heaven.
3. Give us this day our daily bread.
4. Forgive us for our sins as we forgive those who sin against us.
5. Lead us not into temptation; deliver us from the evil one, for yours is the Kingdom and the power and glory forever, Amen!

Let me unpack each line with you!

1. Praise God for who He is, not what He does for you!

When I start to pray in the morning on my way to work, I reach my hand over and act like my Dad is in the car with me and say, Good morning Dad! Then I spend a few minutes praising Him for His eternal qualities. Not for what He's done for me lately. To "hallow" someone is to honor or lift up as sacred. I say, praise your holy name, you alone are faithful, loving, just, pure, and righteous. You are the creator and sustainer, healer and provider, you alone are good, and you alone are God! Thank you for salvation through your son Jesus Christ, for forgiving me and sealing my eternity in heaven with you forever! Thank you for gifting me with your Holy Spirit to change my dark, prideful, lustful, selfish heart into the man you made me to be! I start by thanking God for these truths and many more. It's all about His character and generosity!

Jesus starts by making sure our mindset is right. The Alpha and Omega, beginning, and end, all-powerful, all-knowing, omnipresent. Before I tackle my day, I speak out loud declaring that I live for and have inside of me the One who makes all things possible.

I'll be honest; as a guy, I used to be horrible at being able to praise God for His eternal qualities. As a guy who likes to conquer the next hill, I'm onto praying about what's next. My wife and I like to take walks together. We will pray out loud as we walk. We say, let's tell God how thankful we are for Him and praise Him. I would say, thank you for giving me my wife, kids, provision, allowing to lead someone to Christ, land a big contract. I would list things and then be done.

My wife would spend the next 10 minutes focused on God's eternal qualities as a loving heavenly Father and refer to scriptural truths about who God is. Your mercy is new every morning! You are my rock! She understands the heart of her Father! Dyan taught me how to praise God for who He is, not just what He does for me! Connecting on a personal, heart, emotional level is what Jesus meant!

2. Surrender & Obedience

Line two is about surrender and obedience, rare qualities in our society, but the foundation of any strong relationship; because these two character traits more than anything else build trust. Trust is what anchors you and produces incredible results. See, when you trust someone you listen and follow. Things go smoother and often quicker, even if it's challenging. They are bi-products of love.

When you know someone loves you, it's not a fight, because you know they have your best interest in mind. I settled this one a long time ago that I don't question God's heart. He's proven himself over and over again every generation, and to me, so my posture is I will do whatever and go wherever today so lead me! I have learned to never say no to God. It's always yes. I don't need to know what is going to happen, because I won't understand anyway.

So here's how I unpack this part in my prayer time. Lord, do your will through world leaders, national, state, and local. We are commanded to pray for our leaders, like them or not. Pray for your boss, president, pastors. Scripture is clear that God puts people in positions of authority. Yes, even non-Christians, even evil people. In the story of Moses leading God's people out of slavery in Egypt, God raised up Pharaoh and hardened his heart so he could show his power. Romans chapter 9 talks about God's sovereign right as the potter to mold the clay for honorable and dishonorable use so that He can show His power and mercy. We are so quick to judge God's character, yet our motives even at their best are often laced with selfish needs for security or significance.

How arrogant that we would think we understand all of the layers which lead God to do as He wills. We claim all kinds of truths about what God is up to, and they all fit our belief system. See our minds' job is to create the life that our deep subconscious desires want. i.e., "This is why my political party is so right." "This is why my perspective is right."

So we desperately need to start each day remembering whose Kingdom we serve. It's not ours, not our nation, not our world, but the real King in Heaven.

After I pray for leaders, then I ask God to bless spiritual leaders around the world, pastors, then for Christians. We're told to pray for our fellow believers, those who are spiritually lost (I name friends), the persecuted, enslaved, the poor. Then I list some by name that are in my sphere of influence. I pray for Derrick and Mercy Banda who lead an orphan care ministry in Africa that we support, I pray for our sponsor child Chrispine. Then I pray for Bob Pearson and Doug Ehrgott who lead Horizon International Ministries, then Dave Sumrall and his family and *iTown*, then Pastor Michael Canada, my pastor at *PCC* and his staff and our elders. I pray for my kids' pastors. I pray for my friends who are pastors.

Then I ask God to do his will through me as a follower. I am a son of God first. I state my commitment to serve God today by choosing to live with joy and confidence. I reject being passive, I accept responsibility, will sacrifice for others, and live with the greater reward of eternal life in mind as I make decisions. I will not be mentally FAT. One of my counselors, Bryan Wright, said most people are mentally FAT! We're lazy with how we think. We Feel, then Act, then later Think what did I do that? He said we need to reverse it and think about what is true first, then take positive action forward and submit my feelings to the truth. That mindset of not being FAT has helped me frame my feelings and emotions to take control of my thinking before I act and regret it later.

I then have some I Am statements I share about myself that have to do with who I know God made and called me to be. I claim those truths about myself and ask for God's favor.

Then I ask God to do his will through me as a husband. I chose to marry Dyan and more important than my happiness is that I am faithful to her. I commit to serve her and love her and ask for God's favor on our marriage.

I have told my kids since they were really little, I love you all and will do anything for you, but mommy is first. I love her the most. I wanted them to know we were a package deal! You become one, it's called unity. This is serious stuff that shows God's character.

Marriage is the strongest imagery God uses in the Bible to describe his character with His son and His devotion to us his people, the church, which He calls His bride. You do your kids a disservice when you put them above your spouse. You teach them that life is all about them, that's a horrible lie to instill in them! Ask most teachers, and they will tell you the worst kids are those who their parents worship! More marriages fail because of this misguided prioritization of devotion than any other reason.

I've heard all the stats about how communication, sex, and money are the root cause of divorce. But here's the truth, you get your priorities right and husbands won't chase after success at work and think providing everything for your kids will make their wife happy, and wives would prioritize time to make sure their husband knows they desire them more than finding their worth in being a mom. I've done a lot of marriage coaching, and this could solve most problems and fights! I always told my kids, when you grow up you're going to leave so mom and I have the rest of our lives together, she came first, and it's staying that way.

Next, I pray for my kids. I ask for wisdom for Dyan and I as we raise our kids, even as we relate to them as grown adults. I name each one, Chelsea, Seth and Luke and included spouses and have prayed for future spouses since they were little. It's been so rewarding to now add Jacob and Emma's names! I ask God to guide them to live for Him and influence their friends for Christ. Then I ask for God's favor and lift up any concerns for each.

Lastly, I pray for my work! Notice the order, World, Self, Spouse, Kids, Work. God loves the world so much he gave us His only son to die for us to save us. Outside of one tiny little spec, everything else in life is not about me! God cares just as much about the people that tick me off as He does about me. My salvation needs to be put into perspective that it's not about me!

It's about God and what He wants to do in this world! Then I pray for myself because you can only give out of what you have. Love others the way you love yourself. I must make sure I am filled up so I can give to others. I know a lot of well-meaning Christians who over-commit themselves and stress everyone else out in the name of loving people and being Christ to others. That doesn't impress people or God. That's more about my own need to be the savior! Not my job! Remember, my name is Fred, and I'm your friend! Prioritize your heart so you can lead well!

Remember, when I shared with you the truth I discovered, from Andy Stanley's book, Choosing not to Cheat. Many people choose to cheat at home, thinking work is more important; I'm providing for my family, so God, please help my family understand and fill in the gaps for me.

NO WAY is God's answer! You can't replace a spouse or a parent. God will never honor that type of prayer because his character is relational first. God lives in perfect unity as a triune God. He takes marriage commitments and parenting very seriously. Our first job is to demonstrate God's character relationally through our marriage and then to train up the next generation to learn about who God is by guiding them and loving them.

There will always be more work to do tomorrow. Setting healthy boundaries of time and asking God to fill in the gaps at work is a prayer He will always answer with help! I committed to working no more than 50 hours a week, Biblically speaking six days then a day off. Morning till dinner time. Work hard, give your best and learn to delegate and trust others. I made sure I was home more nights than I was not. I prioritized Saturdays for family, especially since I worked on Sundays. However great an impact God wants me to have in 50hrs, I am good with, because if I cheat my family time, it won't be worth it in the end anyway. Have I made my point clear enough?

So I pray for God to use me at work as a business owner. I pray blessings for my team and their families and that they would add value to others in the work we do. I pray blessings for our clients. I ask God to use me to reach people for Christ. I ask for God's favor financially so I can use those resources to provide for my family and further His Kingdom here on earth. I pray for my students, their parents, and the staff at our school and our administration. I pray for the players I coach and the staff I work with. When I was a pastor, I prayed for my church. I also serve as an elder at our church and ask God to use me in that role.

3. Provision

This is usually why people pray; it's usually the longest part of our prayers. This has actually become my shortest part of my prayer time. I have so much to praise Him for and thank Him for and spend a lot of time surrendering my will to His that when I come to provision, I just know He's got me! So I'm usually pretty short and to the point. I'm not trying to bargain with Him to do what I want or change people. I ask for things and trust He knows best and move on!

This section is where we present our request, needs to God. Side note, I can't ask God for anything until I first thank Him for the ways He has abundantly provided in my life. So here is where I say thank you for my businesses and Dyan's job and our health and family and friends and church, and then I ask Him for specific needs. I am very specific. Pray general prayers, and get general answers. Pray specific and receive specific answers. He already knows what you're wanting and wrestling with, so be honest.

One more little side note, if I want something, whether it's financial, physical or relational, I ask then move on trusting that I will receive it. If it's not happening, I find one of three things happens. I either need to just keep believing and working at it, and it will come in due time. Or if I find myself getting frustrated a lot, then I need to adjust my attitude because what I want is either not good for me or I'm going about it all wrong. And most of the time, once I adjust my attitude, I tend to receive the blessing in the financial situations or in the relationship I was struggling in or the physical situation.

4. Forgiveness

Oh my, haven't I already explained to you how deeply important relationships are to God? The reason Jesus put this in our prayers is so we can have a way to heal rubs daily, so they don't grow into open wounds that infect us and others negatively.

As your friend, listen very carefully to what I'm about to say next because your life depends upon it! After Jesus explained how to pray, the very next sentence in vs. 14 He says if you forgive others, God will forgive you. If you don't forgive others, God won't forgive you! Plain and simple! You bind yourself if you bind others! Remember, I'm your friend. I love you and want the best for you. Don't go to bed angry; don't go to your grave holding back forgiveness.

See, Jesus knew that when we get hurt, our mind fixates on the pain someone caused us and it traps us so that we view everything from that lens. It eats away at our heart. It shuts down our creative capacity; it weakens us. God's enemy, who is real, is hell-bent on destroying your life. Satan is everything that God is not. The scriptures say that he is prowling around like a lion seeking to devour you. The reason Satan always lies and tries to trick us is because his fate is set. The scriptures teach that Satan was the lead angel that used to serve God, and he decided to defy God and tried to take Him out. He misled other angels, and God defeated his attack. He chose not to trust God and received what he wanted, his own authority and Kingdom. It's referred to as the Kingdom of Darkness, God's Kingdom is Light. He was banished from the heavens to earth along with his followers (demons). The opposite of heaven is hell.

The truth is there is a real battle going on for your soul. Life is so much bigger than what we can see. The invisible is what sustains the physical. Science shows this in all of nature's laws. Gravity (invisible) keeps humans (physical) from floating into space and dying. Oxygen (invisible) allows our lungs to provide nutrients for our blood to sustain our organs and systems (physical).

This is not scary, weird spiritual stuff; this is obviously true. We know there is good and evil (invisible spiritual forces), and we know our actions are driven by our thoughts and beliefs. They produce good or bad results (physical realities). Come on, people, why are we so fascinated with movies about the spiritual war between good and evil and keep paying to watch it over and over? Because we know deep down, there is a God that is good and an eternal reward of heaven and an evil enemy and an eternal condemnation of hell. Our conscience and the laws of nature scream it to us every day!

Forgiveness heals us! Forgiveness saved us! Forgiveness restores us! It's God's gift to us! I have decided that I am going to forgive myself and others fast! Immediately, in fact!

I have wasted way too many days, letting what someone said take root in my mind and heart and grow to where it ruins my life. So let me help you learn how to forgive quickly. It doesn't mean you were okay with what someone did. It doesn't mean you are letting them off the hook. It means you are not letting what they said or did to continue to hurt them keep hurting you by choosing to replay it over and over again in your mind.

Friends, most of our pain in life is self-inflicted wounds. Insecurities that we can't get over and keep feeding. If someone keeps hurting you, forgive them, then set a healthy boundary, so you don't keep putting yourself in that position. Now, listen carefully to this next statement, if you don't genuinely forgive and let the pain go first, you can't set healthy boundaries! Trust me, I'm your friend, and I have your best interests in mind! Forgiveness is not an option; it's a command; it will save your life!

I used to spend a lot of time praying for people to change. I now just forgive them and ask for wisdom to see what I can learn and thank God for forgiving me and ask Him to show me how I can change for the better!

5. Preparing for Today's Battle, time to kick some ass!

The last line of Jesus' prayer is like a classic coach or warriors speech before the team or soldiers go out to battle. It's asking for protection from our weaknesses, our temptations. It's asking for deliverance, victory from our evil enemy. Then can you hear the roar of the crowd saying, Yours is the Kingdom, and the Power, and the Glory forever! Amen! I will fight for you my King, I trust you, coach, you know best, you've prepared us, you're spirit of confidence and strength is in me and today will live in glory! It's already done, so let's go claim the victory!

Great coaches and leaders help their followers see and believe in the vision and themselves ahead of time so they can step out with courage and do whatever it takes to succeed.

We get this! But unfortunately, most of the time, these speeches that inspire us to complete devotion are for our glory, to build our little kingdom! So let me share with you how I unpack this section of the prayer: I go into warrior mode.

One of the things I love about God is that He calls Himself a warrior. As an athlete who loves to compete, this imagery speaks to my heart, especially as a man. God created men to display his power and strength, so it could be used to defend and protect others. We are supposed to fight for our wives and kids. We are to go out into the world standing strong against all evil defending the truth. So how do we do this?

This is where memorizing God's word comes in! It's battle preparation! Just as if you don't practice or study you can't perform as well in the game or test because you didn't prepare and can't recall what you don't know. This is why studying the Bible is so important. We pray scripture to overcome negative mindsets that counter God's truth. We face our enemy head-on and put into practice as safeguards that protect us from temptations.

We all know the areas we are weak in, so create a game plan of how to avoid those situations and find mentors who have overcome the same struggles to hold you accountable. Some advice, don't ask your friend who struggles with the same weakness to help you, it never works! You both end up not going to the gym and eating a whole tub of ice cream. You both end up gossiping about how bad your boss is. Trust me on this one!

Tell your real enemy (it's not your spouse or boss), Satan, to get out of your way. You have that kind of authority. Then quote scriptures that speak to your heart and build your obedience. Start putting on the full armor of God: the helmet of salvation (protect your mind, you are loved), the breastplate of righteousness (do the right thing), the shield of faith to distinguish the enemies darts (don't let negative, critical words in), the sword of the spirit (know God's spirit is with you empowering you), the belt of truth (God's word and promises), ready your feet (go share the gospel).

Here are a few scriptures I quote every day at the end of my prayer as preparation for the day's battle:

Romans 8:11 *I am more than a conqueror! I have the spirit that raised Jesus Christ from the dead in me!*

Philippians 4:13 *I can do all things through Christ who gives me strength!*

Romans 8:1 *There is no condemnation for those in Christ Jesus.*

Romans 8:28 *All things work together for the good of those who love the Lord.*

Jeremiah 29:11 *I know the plans I have for you, plans to prosper you and not to harm you!*

Proverbs 3:3-5 *I trust in the Lord with all my heart, I don't lean on my our own understanding, in all my ways I acknowledge the Lord, and he makes my paths straight!*

Philippians 4:4-8 *Rejoice in the Lord always and again I say rejoice! The Lord is near, be anxious about nothing, but through prayer and petition offer your requests to the Lord with thanksgiving and the peace that passes all understanding will guard your heart and mind in Christ Jesus.*

I Corinthians 4:4-8 *Love is patient, love is kind, it does not envy, it's not proud, it keeps no record of wrongs. It* *does not delight in evil but rejoices in the truth. Love always protects, always trusts, always hopes, always perseveres. Love never fails!*

John 14:6 *Jesus said I am the way, the truth, and the life; no one comes to the Father except through the son.*

Joshua 1:9 *Haven't I commanded you? Be strong and courageous! Do not be afraid or discouraged; the Lord, your God, is with you wherever you go. I've already given you the land, go possess it!*

The last one is my personal favorite scripture that I quote every day when I pray! I love Joshua, he was a warrior and had faith when no one else did, and he believed God had already won the battle for him, so it was his to walk into victoriously!

I walk into every interaction with people believing that God has already prepared things for me and that God is going to accomplish more than I could ever imagine! Things don't always go the way I think they will go, but the majority of the time what I trust God for eventually happens! Mindset, my friends! I believe with the core of my being what God says about Himself and me! And God says His word will never return void! So I have decided to focus on learning and living out his word, and this guarantees me victory!

I ask God to use me to help people turn their lives over to Christ every day! And it happens regularly because it's God's heart and it's what I want. So we are on the same page!

Get on God's page. Learn to pray the way Jesus taught us to! Flesh it out with your own words and scriptures, and then enjoy the journey with him!

LESSON 4: FACE IT HEAD ON IMMEDIATELY!

Avoidance delays the inevitable. It also drains energy. It takes more work to avoid things than deal with them. I have found when I have difficult conversations or situations I need to solve, the quicker I work to get on the solution side, the better I handle it, and the more productive my thoughts go.

Fear shuts down our brain's capacity to function. Medically our brain sends messages by releasing chemicals that put us into a state of flight. So our creative abilities are blocked so all attention can be ready to attack. This is great when we need to protect ourselves from serious harm, but this is very damaging if it's our mindset for dealing with anything we're afraid of or uncomfortable with.

My wife and I went to the Bahamas for our 5th wedding anniversary. We went with her sister Suzi and Suzi's husband, Stuart. They got married three months before we did. I already mentioned the close connection Suzi, and I had going through cancer together, and both of us being high energy people lovers! Stuart is one of a kind! He is a rare blend of military drill sergeant and comedian! He really knows how to get both Dyan and Suzi worked up in a Euchre game!

He and I actually became the Euchre champions of the Universe on that trip coming back from being down -15 points to the girls 33pts. They only needed 3 points to win, and the old mojo started working in our favor and let's just say that the ladies didn't appreciate his commentary! In fact, Suzi was so worked up that she separated their twin beds that last night, and he slept feeling her cold vibes!

While we were on the trip, we decided to go to a deserted island for the day! We took a ship over in the morning, and they made it clear to make sure and be back by 5 pm, or you were on your own all night! We had a lot of fun, snorkeling and laying on the beach! Stuart and I decided to go out snorkeling one more time before the end of the day. We went a little way out to a coral reef and didn't see anything, so we kept going out a little further and a little further. It had probably been over 30 minutes, so we decided we better head in. Stuart went to adjust his mask and got a couple of gulps of salt water and was getting tired from all day in the sun. So he started swimming on his back, and I realized that he was swimming in circles, so I started to push his side to keep him straight, and he stopped and yelled, stop touching me! I said you're swimming in circles, so if you don't let me help we're not getting back! After that, I tried to keep him on a straight line without interfering with his arms.

Then Stuart let go of the mask he was holding so he could swim more easily. I saw it floating to the bottom, and I took a deep breath to go get it, and right then Stuart asked, "Are we there yet?" For a split second, I was overwhelmed with the reality that we might die! We had just started swimming. We had a long way to go! Stuart was a former athlete, so he was in good shape, he's 6'2" and probably weighed around

215lbs, and even though he was in the Navy, he is not very buoyant. I, on the other hand, weighed 150lbs. I thought to myself there is no way I can help carry him back! So forget the mask!

I said, just keep going! We didn't realize how far out we had gone. I'm not sure how far out we were, but all I knew was when the waves went up you couldn't see the island and they were taking us out, not in.

We had to work hard against the current. Every 30 seconds, Stuart would ask, "Are we there yet?" And I would say, "A little further, just keep going." This went on for probably close to an hour! Once we got in shallow enough to stand, I told him you're good. I walked out to see if we had missed the boat since I didn't see anyone on the shore and when I turned back to look Stuart had fallen back into the water, he was exhausted! Just then, Dyan and Suzi came running and said, "Where have you been? Hurry the boat is leaving!" Stuart then said to Suzi, "Honey, you and kids flashed before my eyes!" That was scary!

I don't know if you've ever had a life-threatening situation, but we can all identify with the fear that comes over us when we don't know what to do and especially if we are worn out!

Stuart and I had a choice to make at that moment. We didn't have time to talk about it. We both decided to focus on what we could do and just keep taking the next step believing we could make it back. Friends, the difference between success and failure is not whether or not you are afraid. It's what you do when you experience times of fear and discouragement. NEVER let fear stop you!

Do you know how many times God addresses fear in the Bible? Over 500 times! Why does God talk about how to deal with fear so much? Because He knows it's a natural tendency for us to worry or doubt. Catch this, do you know how many times God talks about faith in the Bible? Over 750 times, God talks about having faith or believing! That's how much He talks about love also! We all know that we talk a lot about what's important to us! If you want to know what someone is thinking about just listen to what they say all the time!

Friends, God loves you, and He believes in you and wants you to have faith in Him and yourself! If there is one thing I would encourage you to master in life, it would be to learn the truth that fear is overrated! It has never accomplished anything; it only controls and intimidates and destroys whoever believes in it.

So how do you keep fear from taking root in your life? Take action! Don't stop! Keep moving forward. Faith and courage are not void of fear and doubt. They are simply the antidote! Try it! The next time you are afraid, just keep pushing, take the next step. Tell yourself fear can only kill me if I let it, so since I'm in full control of what I believe, choose to think about what you can do and confidently do it!

Most people are deathly afraid of public speaking! So the advice most people give when someone is nervous is to take a deep breath and calm down.

If you study the way the brain processes, this is not the best advice. To tell someone to calm down is a rational approach; fear and worry are irrational, emotional responses. It's better to meet emotion with emotion. As a public speaker, you want energy, so you don't bore people. So Roddy Galbraith, my speaking coach through the John Maxwell Team, says it like this, three simple words said out loud are the best response if you feel nervous or if someone asks you how you feel about your talk? I am excited!

There have been scientific studies done that show when you channel your emotion of fear into positive thought, it causes all of your brain synapses to fire at full speed and allows you to access your most creative thinking! Fear paralyzes and shuts down, so meet it with emotion, not logic and take action. The best way to conquer fear is to act, not to try to reason it out. Think about the time you were afraid to jump off that cliff, the more you thought about it, the bigger your fear grew, but when you just did it anyways the thrill was a rush, and you end up with a feeling of strength that you pushed through!

So learn to master fear by taking whatever positive action you can! That's all, just take the next step, don't worry about the 2nd, 3rd, or 4th step, when you get to those steps just take the next step again forward. And before you know it, you will have arrived at a new place that leaves you feeling more confident and ready to tackle the next hurdle you have to face. Because you do know how life works don't you? Once you face your fears, there is another challenge that's bigger, a place you've never been, and each time you push through and work that faith muscle it gets stronger and can handle more!

So learn to realize that God is testing you because He believes in you and wants to help you grow stronger! But if you choose to shrink back in fear, the next challenge you face will feel overwhelming even if it's not that big of a challenge. We've all been around people that make a mountain out of a molehill. Come on, man, why are you so worried? If you stop working the faith muscle, your mind grows weak and can't handle the small stuff.

And one other thing about fear and faith, whatever you fear and let stop you is in direct proportion to how you experience God's power. So every time you shrink back, God gets smaller in your mind, and you get angrier and more defeated and find yourself blaming God. Your faith in yourself either expands your view of God or reduces it. This is really important to understand! Some Christians have a very hard time separating their faith in themselves and their faith in God. They say things like, I believe God can do anything but then qualify that with a statement that sounds like humility but is really insecurity speaking. They say, my faith is in God, not myself, or they are critical of people who lead with confidence or that stand up for themselves and have the courage to confront people. I often hear people say someone is prideful or not very nice, and it's more about their own fears or insecurities.

As I study the scriptures, I am confident that leaders like the Apostle Paul, King David, Ruth, and Jesus would have been labeled as arrogant and prideful by many Christian today if they lived back then. The reason I know this is because those people were accused of those things. These men and women were confident, strong, definitive, and persistent; and they accomplished incredible things for God.

There is one thing I've learned to discern in my 50 years; it's to know when someone is masking their fears as concerns or spirituality maturity. People who criticize and complain about others regularly do so out of their own low self-worth. And if called on it, they would never admit that they are struggling with feeling less than and therefore need to put someone else down to feel better about themselves. Instead, they make you feel bad for even suggesting it and then use shame to try to make you feel bad and become over spiritual.

You see, we tend to be most critical in others about the things we struggle with. It's our way of protecting our image. We don't even realize that we do this! Remember, my name is Fred, and I'm your friend! Never let someone else's fear or criticism or spiritual righteousness cause you to think less of yourself! If you want to see God work as powerfully as he did in Biblical days, then you're going to have to spend a lot of time in the gym every day exercising your own faith! God matches your faith with His power.

Moses had to first step into the sea before it was parted. David was the first one to step up and face Goliath's taunting of how weak God was, and finally, the power of God was seen when he defeated the giant. Paul had to boldly tell the sick and nonbelievers that healing and forgiveness are found in Jesus Christ, and lives were changed.

If you wait for God to act first, you won't see God! Faith without deeds is dead! There is no such thing as belief without action! This is why God went first to demonstrate His love for you by dying for you on a cross! When you know you are loved, it drives out fear and moves you into action!

Can I say something that might sting a little here? Husbands, do whatever it takes to make sure your wife knows that you love her more than your work or possessions. Cherish her always! And wives, give your best to your husband, not your kids! He needs your love and support more than you will ever know! When we love our spouse in the way that meets their need, it helps build self-worth and confidence. Let's not tear each other down out of our own fears!

Face your fears immediately every day, because it's how your faith in God and yourself grows.

If you would like to see where you're at in living by faith take my Faith Survey on my website **www.Fred-Talk.com,** then check out the resources I have to help you grow your faith in God, Yourself and Others!

LESSON 5: MENTAL MASTERY

What if it comes back? Pessimists always focus on what if's, making it sound like they are being wise or caring. Never spend one moment worrying about the things that you cannot control. When planning in life, it's good to think through potential problems and how you will address them. Intentional learning is always better than learning the hard way! But intentional worrying teaches us nothing and only grows more worries. Worry never solves anything!

As I began writing this book on vacation in northern Michigan on Torch Lake, I started experiencing some swelling in my right groin and tenderness. That's where I had my lymphadenectomy. I had been learning how to wake surf and felt like I may have strained my groin after a long run, it kept persisting a week after I came home, so I decided to call the doctor and have it checked out just to be proactive.

They had me do some CT scans, and I met with my Oncologist. My wife asked me if I was nervous and I said no because I didn't think it is anything major, but if it was, we would catch it and deal with it.

I have a firm belief that God will use everything in my life for good and I don't sense He's done with me yet. The only thing I can't control is that I will die, that will be a good day to get to meet my maker face to face and thank Him for his amazing grace on my life, but until then, there's work to do and people to love!

So I saw this as an opportunity to share with my doctors that I wrote a book, they are in it and asked them to help me get it into the hands of every cancer patient they know so we can breathe hope into people! There is a difference between planning out of fear, so something bad doesn't happen and planning from a place of growth and character. When you genuinely trust God's heart, it doesn't matter what you have to face, scary or not. I found out that my swollen groin was a hernia, so I'm working to heal it up and will have surgery if needed!

The truth, that you can face scary and unknown things with confidence if you know God's heart, reminds me of the time when I was in High School and the story of the Blue Gremlin. One of my best friends from High School lived an hour away. Jerry Klinesmith's dad was also a pastor, and we grew up knowing each other from church camp. We would see each other a few times a year. Then when we got our license, we started driving to each other's house most months.

We both lived out in the country, so not a lot of cars. So we had this thing we did where if we saw each other coming down our road we would cross on the other side of the street. I know that sounds really stupid and dangerous! Now come on, I'm supposed to be your friend! I really cannot remember where we got the idea from or who suggested it. I think it just happened one day goofing around.

Well, Jerry had a Blue Gremlin. If you don't know what that is you are missing out of one of the real classics of all time cars! They were made by AMC and were kind of like a Ford Pinto, another classic! Google them just for fun. They always had classic 60's hippie colors! You could spot this car from a mile away! And Jerry always went first; I would be driving down the road not paying attention, and then all of a sudden see a car swerve in my lane, and I would get a big grin on my face and start chuckling!

Well, one day, my mom was in the car with me, and yep, Jerry's blue Gremlin came crossing over into my lane. You can imagine the look on my mom's face! She had no idea what was going on! She screamed, "Freddie, what is that car doing?"

In a moment, everything flashed before my eyes! I thought oh no, crap, my dad is going to find out and I'm dead! I calmly reached my hand over and said to my mom, just trust me! Then I proceeded to cross over to the other side of the road and passed Jerry while he just smiled and waved at us! That time Jerry was the one chuckling! Then I explained to my mom what had just happened, and to my surprise, she didn't say a word to my dad or me! In fact, to this day when I ask her about it, she doesn't remember it! I think she was so scared that it just got blocked out of her memory!

Yes, we do some pretty foolish things growing up! But give me a little leeway here and hang with me as I stretch things like any good youth pastor can with a story like this! There are a lot of things in life that seem foolish and scary to us. But if you are on the inside and know what's really happening it's not near as foolish or scary as you think it is! I wasn't afraid; I knew exactly what was going on and what to do. I had done it dozens of times before! So when I said, just trust me, my mom was safe, and I had her best interests in mind when I proceeded to cross over and drive on the wrong side of the road! Are you following me? Do you see where this is going yet?

God has been doing things that we may never understand for generations, He knows exactly what He's doing, and every generation thinks they know what's best, what's right, what's safe. The Bible says that God's ways are not like our ways; they are so much higher. When you fly in a plane, you get a whole different perspective of life. God's at an altitude that blows aways our best SAT score or Intelligence test or net worth! He sees it all! He owns it all! So just relax!

You will never be able to know or see what's next. Even the best plans must make room for midcourse corrections due to unforeseen circumstances. Some of us handle changes better than others because of our wiring. So here is my best advice for life, learn to Master Your Mind!

Work hardest on growing yourself, becoming deeply aware of who you are, what drives you, scares you, and always be in a state of thinking about what you're thinking about. In other words, know why you feel what you're feeling and why you do what you do. Mastery is knowing the whys and learning how to identify accurately and habitually produce what you want.

So let me unpack what I just said with a few examples. The best athletes prepare mentally and physically, they know their strengths and weaknesses and plan ahead, when things are not going as planned they quickly seek advice from their coach and identify what is not working and make adjustments. They don't get stuck in feelings of frustration, quickly forget mistakes while learning from them, and keep their focus on the goal. They never get mentally lazy! They are intentional with their time, what they eat, their sleep; they submit themselves to the processes, and people that will produce the results they want. When we watch them compete it looks effortless, like a machine, it's a thing of beauty! This mastery only comes in direct proportion to the investment made on the front end!

This idea of mental mastery is what the Apostle Paul talks about in Romans 12:2, where he explains how to transform your mind to produce good fruit that lasts. *Don't become so well-adjusted to your culture that you fit into it without even thinking. Instead, renew your mind by fixing your attention on God. You'll be changed from the inside out. Readily recognize what he wants from you, and quickly respond to it. Unlike the culture around you, always dragging you down to its level of immaturity, God brings the best out of you, develops well-formed maturity in you.* (MESS)

You are the master of only one life, but if you work at it diligently you will be able to persuade and influence others in positive ways that will produce incredible results together, but it all starts with mastery. If you don't work at it your circumstances, money, and people will master you. So stop trying to control others, stop trying to play God, focus your attention on your mindset. Everything else falls into place if we are thinking well! In Philippians 4, after Paul talks about setting our mindset straight by remembering that God is with us and listens to our prayers. He talks about being thankful and how there is a peace that transcends all understanding that comes from Christ. Then in the very next verse 8, he says, think about whatever is true, noble, right, pure, lovely, admirable, excellent, praiseworthy, think about such things! Think about what you think about!

You didn't create yourself or this world, you didn't get to decide when you were born or where, you don't know what tomorrow brings or when you will die. Those things are all set for us. They were not random; they were meticulously planned out ahead of time for a very unique purpose. Find your purpose! Connect with your creator! Discover who you are! Then live out of that security. It frees you to not have to know everything, to not have to believe everything people say about you or life.

When you understand that self-control is not about knowing everything, but rather knowing what is going on inside of you so that you can produce what you want externally no matter what things look like, then life is simple, peaceful, fulfilling. And out of this calmness of spirit, we find strength and power to face whatever is next in life!

There is a song most people have heard that says, "Jesus, take the wheel." But God never intended that we would not be in the driver's seat of our life. He has given us our life to live, chosen wisely, we use it to glorify our Creator.

Learning how to master our actions, by mastering our emotions, by mastering our thoughts, which come from our beliefs … that process honors God because it demonstrates to the world that we understand what life is all about and shows that we have been good stewards of what God entrusted us with.

We were created in God's image to reflect His character; mastery of ourselves allows us to be consistent in our responses to life, producing fruit that is positive and lasts. Then one day, when we all stand before our Creator, we will be able to hear the words every child wants to hear from their loving father, well done my good and faithful servant. I am very pleased with you! You have shown yourself trustworthy with a small thing; now, I will put you in charge of greater things. Come enjoy life everlasting with me!

We don't earn a father's love; it's given. When we know and receive that we are loved then out of that security, we can live confidently by faith and produce goodness as a result. It's how our world comes to know the ONE and ONLY TRUE GOD!

So how did I overcome cancer, depression, and a career change in my mid 40's? By the grace of God working through me to reflect his love and power and beauty! I can't take any credit for it, but I am responsible for what I become and do.

So I challenge you to live your life worthy of the calling you have been given! Remember, I'm Fred, and I'm your friend. I hope you are smiling.

I believe in you, my friend, and so does your creator, so go show off God's goodness and power to our world!

Special Thanks:

To my kids ... I love seeing each of you live out who God made you to be uniquely! I see God working powerfully in each of you!

Chelsea, for being my favorite daughter! I love your positive, fun spirit and how everything is always the best ever! I love dreaming with you, and you have been a huge blessing administratively and with advertising as I've developed my businesses! I also love watching you lead others with your heart! You inspire me!

Seth, for being a man of conviction! I love your passion for life! You make us laugh, love your impersonations! I am so proud of how hard you work at your goals for your career, health, and relationships! I knew you were a leader early, and I love to watch you influence people by stepping up, speaking up and doing the right thing! You inspire me!

Luke, for being your own person, Lkue! I love how confident you are in your own skin and how you think through things and handle pressure well! You are a strong leader by example, and people listen when you choose to say something! I love watching you excel at football and seeing you care for people and push them to be better! Cholondo! You inspire me!

Devin, for being my editor and publisher! I couldn't have finished all the details without your expertise! I am the run-on King! You are a gifted leader and have great vision for what works! Thanks for leading the way by writing and publishing your own books! It's been an easy process working together! You inspire me!

NOTES:

Section One

1. Matthew 21:21
2. *"Biology of Belief,"* Bruce Lipton – pg 122
3. *"As a Man Thinketh,"* James Allen – pg 8
4. *"As a Man Thinketh,"* James Allen – pg 8
5. *"As a Man Thinketh,"* James Allen – pg 14
6. *"Biology of Belief,"* Bruce Lipton – prologue xiv

Section Two

7. Joshua 1:9
8. Exodus 16:4
9. Exodus 16:35

Made in the
USA
Lexington, KY